Global India circa 100 CE

South Asia in Early World History

Key Issues in Asian Studies, No. 5

AAS Resources for Teaching About Asia

Global India circa 100 CE

South Asia in Early World History

Richard H. Davis

Association for Asian Studies, Inc.
1021 East Huron Street
Ann Arbor, MI 48104 USA
www.asian-studies.org

KEY ISSUES IN ASIAN STUDIES
A series edited by Lucien Ellington, University of Tennessee at Chattanooga

"Key Issues" booklets complement the Association for Asian Studies teaching journal, *Education About Asia*—a practical teaching resource for secondary school, college, and university instructors, as well as an invaluable source of information for students, scholars, libraries, and those who have an interest in Asia.

Formed in 1941, **the Association for Asian Studies (AAS)**—the largest society of its kind, with more than 7,000 members worldwide—is a scholarly, non-political, non-profit professional association open to all persons interested in Asia.

For further information, please visit www.asian-studies.org

For orders or inquiries, please contact:

Association for Asian Studies, Inc.
1021 East Huron Street
Ann Arbor, Michigan 48104 USA
Tel: (734) 665-2490; Fax: (734) 665-3801
www.asian-studies.org

Library of Congress Cataloging-in-Publication Data

Davis, Richard H.
Global India circa 100 CE : South Asia in early world history / Richard H. Davis.
    p. cm. — (Key issues in Asian studies ; no. 5)
    Includes bibliographical references.
    ISBN 978-0-924304-59-0 (pbk. : alk. paper) 1. India—Civilization—To 1200. 2. India—Relations—Foreign countries. 3. India—Civilization—To 1200—Foreign influences. I. Title.
    DS425.D373 2009
    303.48'234009015—dc22

                              2009046212

Cover Photo: Statue of Kumarajiva at Kizlin Grotto, Xinjiang. Source: iStockphoto.com

ABOUT THE AUTHOR

RICHARD H. DAVIS is Professor of Religion and Asian Studies at Bard College, Annandale on-Hudson, NY. Previously he taught at Yale University. He is author of three books: *Ritual in an Oscillating Universe: Worshiping Siva in Medieval India* (Princeton University Press, 1991); *Lives of Indian Images* (Princeton University Press, 1997; winner of the 1999 AAS Ananda Kentish Coomaraswamy Book Prize); and *A Priest's Guide to the Great Festival: Aghorasiva's Mahotsavavidhi* (Oxford University Press, 2009). He has also edited two volumes: *Images, Miracles, and Authority in Asian Religious Traditions* (Westview Press, 1998); and *Picturing the Nation: Iconographies of Modern India* (Orient Longman, 2006). He has served in several capacities with the Association for Asian Studies (AAS), as a member of the AAS South Asia Council (SAC) and as an Associate Editor for the *Journal of Asian Studies* (*JAS*). He is currently working on a cultural history of early South Asia and on a study of the history of the *Bhagavad Gita*.

About "Key Issues in Asian Studies"

Key Issues in Asian Studies (**KIAS**) is a series of booklets engaging major cultural and historical themes in the Asian experience. *KIAS* booklets complement the Association for Asian Studies teaching journal, *Education About Asia*, and serve as vital educational materials that are both accessible and affordable for classroom use.

KIAS booklets tackle broad subjects or major events in an introductory but compelling style appropriate for survey courses. Although authors of the series have distinguished themselves as scholars as well as teachers, the prose style employed in *KIAS* booklets is accessible for broad audiences. This series is particularly intended for teachers and undergraduates at two- and four-year colleges as well as advanced high school students and secondary school teachers engaged in teaching Asian studies in a comparative framework.

For further information about *Key Issues in Asian Studies* booklets, *Education About Asia*, or the Association for Asian Studies, please visit www.asian-studies.org.

Prospective authors interested in *Key Issues in Asian Studies* or *Education About Asia* are encouraged to contact:

Lucien Ellington
University of Tennessee at Chattanooga
Tel: (423) 425-2118
Fax (423) 425-5441
E-Mail: Lucien-Ellington@utc.edu
www.asian-studies.org/EAA

Editor's Introduction

One of the most mistaken stereotypes about South Asian civilizations is that they, in contrast to the "dynamic" west, have been static throughout the centuries. In this engaging booklet, Richard Davis effectively refutes this misimpression of South Asia. He also, in the process, assists instructors and students in gaining a perspective on globalization informed by a better knowledge of early world history.

Richard does much more than the above. This booklet is a wonderful story as well as an educational tool. Real-life—as well as mythical—people tell the stories of their interactions and perceptions of the "other" during the course of the story. Greeks, Romans, South and Central Asians and Chinese all make appearances. We hear the accounts, and share the stories of scholars, holy men, political leaders, merchants, and warriors and these experiences collectively deepen our understanding of cross-cultural connections and perceptions so long ago. It seems that for over a century, too many academic historians have often neglected rendering accounts of individuals in their attempts to help students and the public learn about the past. Ironically, in at least recent years, this somewhat depressing event has occurred amidst clear evidence of the popularity of historical biographies among the reading public. Richard does an excellent job of deftly attending to broad historical narrative brush strokes without neglecting the human factor in the story.

Also, as probably evident by now, Richard makes his story refreshingly "inter-disciplinary" while still producing an interesting and coherent narrative. This booklet will be useful for instructors and students in a wide variety of disciplines and courses including early world history, introduction to South Asia and comparative religion.

My special thanks to Richard, who has, for almost a decade, taught me a great deal about early world history. The booklet would also not have been possible without the helpful comments of Martha Selby, William Harman, and Fritz Blackwell. As always, I am deeply grateful to the AAS Editorial Board, AAS Publications Manager, Jonathan Wilson, and AAS Publications Coordinator, Gudrun Patton for their strong support of pedagogical scholarship projects such as "Key Issues in Asian Studies" and *Education About Asia*.

Lucien Ellington
Series Editor, Key Issues in Asian Studies

Acknowledgements

The instigation for this study came from the challenge of teaching undergraduate courses in early Indian history at Bard College. I would like to thank all my questioning Bard students. They formed my target audience as I wrote this booklet. A sabbatical provided by the college allowed me the time to complete the work, and I thank Bard for its support of faculty research. I also wish to state my appreciation for the Yale University library, my home away from home during my sabbatical.

I am deeply grateful to Lucien Ellington, the series editor for the series *Key Issues in Asian Studies*, whose request set the writing of this booklet in motion. He has been supportive throughout my work on it and made numerous valuable suggestions at every stage of the project. Stewart Gordon provided thoughtful and astute guidance at the start of the work. I would like to thank several others who read drafts and generously gave me more suggestions than I was able to incorporate in this brief booklet: Bradley Clough, Rob Culp, Zilkia Janer, and Kristin Scheible. Rick Asher and Martha Selby helped with references at key moments. I am also grateful to the anonymous readers for the *Key Issues* series, who added valuable suggestions. Finally, I would like to thank Jonathan Wilson and Gudrun Patton at the Association for Asian Studies for their editorial and design assistance.

CONTENTS

ILLUSTRATIONS

TIMELINE

TO THE WEST OF SOUTH ASIA

327 BCE After defeating the Achaemenid empire, Alexander of Macedonia invades as far as the Indus River

305 BCE Seleucus Nicator, Greek satrap ruling in Afghanistan, defeated by Mauryans

197–146 BCE Roman conquest of Greece, leading to dominance in eastern Mediterranean

30 BCE Roman annexation of Egypt

27 BCE–14 CE Reign of Augustus Caesar, establishment of Roman Empire

23–79 CE Life of Pliny the Elder, author of Natural History

70 CE Destruction of Jewish Second Temple in Jerusalem

ca. 70 CE Composition of Periplus Maris Erythraei

247–68 CE Goth attacks on Roman Empire

SOUTH ASIA

563–483 BCE Life of Buddha Shakyamuni

321 BCE Establishment of the Mauryan empire with reign of Chandragupta Maurya

268–233 BCE Reign of Ashoka Maurya

244 BCE Buddhist Council at Pataliputra led by Moggaliputta Tissa

161–137 BCE Reign of Duttagamini in Sri Lanka

160–135 BCE Reign of Menander in northwestern regions

15–65 CE Kujala Kadphises unites Yuezhi regions to form Kushana empire

52 CE Apostle Thomas arrives in southern India (according to tradition)

78–102 CE Reign of Kanishka

81 CE Bala's Buddha image; early Gandhara images of the Buddha

ca. 100 CE Composition of Manu's Dharmashastra

320–550 CE Gupta empire in northern India

EAST AND NORTH OF SOUTH ASIA

209 BCE Establishment of Han dynasty

177–119 BCE Han Chinese conflicts with Xiongnu

102 BCE Chinese general returns from Central Asia with "blood-sweat" horses

57–75 CE Reign of Chinese Emperor Ming

80 CE Chinese chronicles Han-shu

90 CE First Buddhist monastery established in Chinese capital

148 CE An Shih-kao, Buddhist translator, arrives in Lo-yang

ca. 150 CE Establishment of Funan in Southeast Asia

166 CE Cult of the Buddha formally introduced at imperial court in Lo-yang

220 CE End of Han dynasty, beginning of Three Kingdoms period

343–413 CE Lifespan of Kumarajiva

337–422 CE Lifespan of Faxian

INTRODUCTION

SOUTH ASIA IN WORLD HISTORY

I n his book *The White House Years*, former secretary of state Henry Kissinger provides a background lesson on South Asia in his narrative of the India-Pakistan crisis of 1971.

> Bordered on the south by the Indian Ocean, on the north by the Himalayas, and on the west by the Hindu Kush mountains that merge with the heavens as if determined to seal off the teeming masses, and petering out in the east in the marshes and rivers of Bengal, the Indian subcontinent has existed through the millennia as a world apart.[1]

In the view of this influential American diplomat and foreign policy expert, geographical barriers of oceans, mountains, and marshes between South Asia and the rest of the world have led to cultural isolation of the "teeming masses" and a kind of lethargic lack of historical change. The Indian subcontinent, for Kissinger, is separated from the rest of the globe as a "world apart."

Kissinger is not alone in adopting this perspective. He simply repeats a stereotype found in much of the historical scholarship about South Asia and one that continues to appear in many histories of India. Kissinger admits that conquests from outside have occasionally brought new peoples into South Asia, but he asserts that these outsiders have made no fundamental difference in the society as a whole.

> Its polyglot peoples testify to the waves of conquerors who have descended upon it through the mountain passes, from the neighboring deserts, and occasionally from across the sea. Huns, Mongols, Greeks, Persians, Moguls, Afghans, Portuguese, and at last Britons have established empires and then vanished, leaving multitudes oblivious of either the coming or going. (1979: 842)

This "oblivious" attitude is ascribed most often to distinctive (and allegedly unchanging) features of Indian civilization such as the "caste system" and Hinduism. So, Kissinger continues:

The Hindu religion is proud and self-contained; it accepts no converts. One is either born into it or forever denied its comforts and the assured position it confers. Foreign conquest is an ultimate irrelevancy in the face of such impermeability; it gives the non-Indian no status in Indian society, enabling Indian civilization to survive, occasionally even to thrive, through centuries of foreign rule.[2]

For many Western observers, like Kissinger, this depiction invokes a series of contrasts between India and the West, a "strange lop-sided complementarity between the Western Self and its Indian Other," as Ronald Inden puts it (1990: 3). Kissinger implicitly compares the self-contained, oblivious, impermeable India with the outward-looking, dynamic, historically progressive West, embodied here by the modern American diplomat and author.

European, American, and Indian historians and writers have all contributed to this representation. In the period since World War II and the breakup of the old European colonial empires, the American organization of area studies, based on a geographical segmentation of the world into discrete civilizational areas, has institutionalized an intellectual paradigm for the study of the non-Western world that places the greatest value on the intensive study of a single region in isolation. A scholar trained in a South Asian area studies program, such as myself, tends to focus first of all on the inherent character of South Asian cultural forms rather than on the interactions between South Asia with other parts of the world. We may portray the Indian subcontinent in much more nuanced and positive terms than does Kissinger, avoiding his colonial era clichés of "teeming masses" and "waves of conquerors," but we have by and large shared his premise that India can be viewed as a world (or at least a civilization) unto itself.

In recent decades, Hindu nationalist writers in India have pursued this vision of an autonomous India with a vengeance. They argue that India as a predominantly Hindu civilization embodies a cohesive cultural continuity dating back five thousand years give or take a millennium. In this view, extraneous forces may have attacked and at times conquered India militarily, but they have never disrupted or altered the fundamental solidarity of Hindu society and culture (Davis 2004). If Kissinger, with his august condescension to India, sees its unchanging masses as a drag on proper historical development, the Hindu nationalists, in their defensive chauvinism, take great pride in the putative self-sufficiency of Hindu India.

INDIA AND THE WORLD

Whether cast in a negative or positive light, depictions of India as a world apart are historically misleading. From the extensive ancient trade between the earliest world civilizations in Mesopotamia and the Indus Valley in the third millennium BCE right up to the call centers in Bangalore and Hyderabad that take orders from customers in California and Florida for cotton shirts made in Bangladesh and distributed by a company in Maine, some South Asians have always been closely connected to other parts of the world. *Globalization* is a new word, and the underlying conception of the earth as a globe is not one shared by ancient peoples in India or elsewhere. However, the historical reality it points to has always been present. Throughout history, human processes have brought peoples living in different geographical regions into contact with one another for a wide variety of purposes. South Asia has never been separated from that connectedness. There have been changes over time in the speed and quantity of globalizing forces, of course, but the phenomenon itself has been remarkably persistent.

The purpose of this booklet is to survey and illustrate some of the ways India was engaged with other parts of the world during one period in its history, in classical times of roughly the first two centuries of the common era. My argument here is simply that India was not then "a world apart," but rather a complex civilization involved in myriad types of exchanges—of goods, ideas, and peoples—with the surrounding world. Far from being irrelevant to an impermeable Hindu culture, as Kissinger and others might have it, these exchanges sent broad and complicated reverberations throughout Indian society. They have expanded the horizons of the world known to Indians and made India better known throughout the globe. And the consequences of these connections are still with us today in ways both trivial and profound.

In the course of this account I will consider engagements that stretch from the Indian subcontinent outward to the Middle East, the Roman Empire of the Mediterranean Sea, Central Asia, China, and Southeast Asia. I draw on sources ranging from Roman coins found in a South Indian riverbed to an epic poem written in classical Sanskrit.

I have chosen for this depiction a period that I find particularly interesting in the history of global India. During the first two centuries CE, we will see that historical events far beyond South Asia—such as the Roman imperial annexation of Egypt in 30 BCE and the efforts of the Chinese Han empire to extend its boundaries farther west in the first century BCE—contributed to the integration of South Asia into the "world system" of that era. Developments emanating from within the subcontinent, such as the wide-ranging international travels of Buddhist missionaries and the expansion of Aryan cultural forms throughout the subcontinent, were equally important in making India an integral part of the larger world of the early centuries CE. In my view a full account of any period in the history of India would find a similar range of interactions between it and other regions of the world.[3]

FOUR AGENTS OF GLOBALIZATION

In his recent broad overview of the history of globalization, ranging from sixty thousand years ago, when bands of modern *Homo sapiens* first migrated out of their African homelands, up to his present-day purchase of an iPod, Nayan Chanda identifies four primary categories of people who throughout history have pushed forward globalizing developments. While globalization ultimately stems, he writes, "from a basic urge to seek a better and more fulfilling life," it has been driven primarily "by many actors who can be classified, for the sake of simplicity, as traders, preachers, adventurers, and warriors (2007: xi–xii)." Each of these types of globalizing agents may be found in classical India. Through their activities and experiences we can observe the dynamic interactions of the Indian subcontinent with the rest of the world.

Traders, writes Chanda, are "people who produce or carry products and services to consumers in distant parts of the planet and, in the process, have created an interconnected world" (2007: 37). Observing the basic economic adage of "buy low, sell high," traders satisfy consumer needs or desires with goods, and in the exchange they realize a profit for themselves. Trade may involve only local commodities or it may involve the transportation of materials over vast distances, from one part of the world to another, in search of new consumers and markets. It is the latter type of trade in which we will be most interested here. Through their profit-making exchanges, traders introduce not only new goods into an area but also may serve as the bearers of new customs and ideas.

Preachers or missionaries are religious teachers who are driven to seek not profits but converts to another belief or way of life. The sociologist Max Weber defined missionary religion—a category in which he included Buddhism, Christianity, and Islam—as one that "raises the spreading of truth and the conversion of the unbelievers to the rank of a 'sacred duty'" (Chanda 2007: 111). Convinced of the universal applicability and beneficial effects of their faith, missionaries travel beyond their homelands to "convert the unconverted," as the Buddha Sakyamuni put it, wherever those unconverted may be found.

4

Warriors who aim to create or organize larger states or empires through military means may also be agents of globalization. As Chanda observes, "Many motives have driven the creation of empires: ambition to erect God's kingdom on earth, greed for wealth, visions of glory, and universalist political ideals" (2007: 177). Warriors driven by such desires, he continues, have invaded distant lands and brought vast numbers of people of different ethnic, religious, and linguistic groups under their control. The political organization of large polities, then, has the effect of increasing the interconnectedness of previously separate communities under the wider umbrella of empire. It is important to observe here that these categories of agents affect one another. In forming larger political states, empire-building warriors also facilitate trade within the imperial borders and often contribute to the organization of external trade on a broader basis. They may also promote the spread of missionary activities, as we will see.

Finally, "adventurer" is a broad category that includes explorers, travelers, pilgrims, and migrants. Some may be forced to leave their homelands driven by hardship or oppression or they may set out in hopes of finding new opportunities elsewhere. Others may venture forth to learn about lands beyond their own or to visit places they consider holy. They may travel individually or in groups. The separations between Chanda's categories are not always so clear-cut. Missionaries may be adventurers, and as adventurers they may be involved in trade, missionary proselytizing, or military expansion. In this booklet I will look at Rama, the hero of the epic poem *Ramayana*, as an exemplary adventurer who also appears in certain respects as a preacher of Hindu cultural values and as a Kshatriya warrior. In any case, the movements and migrations of such adventurers lead them to new encounters with communities and cultures and thereby contribute to greater human interconnectedness.

The globalizing processes these agents set in motion involve change. They may challenge or disrupt customary ways of doing things. There may be loss as well as gain. As Chanda notes, globalization can provoke anxiety and resistance among those who feel threatened. Just as many in our contemporary world protest the rapid changes brought about by modern forces of globalization (and often with good reason), so, too, in classical India there were some who viewed outsiders with suspicion and disdain and tried to limit or resist the changes instigated by others. In any account of global connections, it is necessary to consider also the responses of those who would prefer the familiar to the exotic, the domestic to the foreign. I will call them "localists." After individual chapters exploring the four agents of globalization, a brief concluding chapter will consider the more conservative responses of Indian localists.

1

TRADERS

In his memoir of growing up in the city of Madurai in the 1940s, Manohar Devadoss tells of an art teacher at his high school who one day shows his students a collection of old coins. Most of them, he explains, are from ancient Rome. "What is special about the coins," the teacher continues, "is that I picked them up from the Vaigai riverbed (1997: 75)." He explains that the best time to search for old coins is after floods subside, when the rushing waters have shifted the sands of the riverbed. The city of Madurai lies inland, along the Vaigai River, in the deep south of India. It is indeed remarkable that a high school teacher and amateur numismatist living there in the mid–twentieth century should have amassed a collection of two-thousand-year-old coins from Rome. Madurai is an ancient city, certainly, but it is over forty-five hundred miles from the imperial capital of the Roman Empire. How did this come about?

The Vaigai riverbed is not the only place in southern India where Roman coins have turned up. Over six thousand have been found in dozens of locations both along the Indian coast and at locations along inland waterways such as Madurai. Archaeologists have uncovered many other items of Roman origin in southern India, including distinctive pottery, jewelry, and glassware. Large amphora, tall, narrow-necked jars widely used by the Romans to transport wine and olive oil, have been unearthed at several places in South India. All of these archaeological finds clearly indicate that in the first few centuries CE there was a significant trade linking southern India and distant Rome.[1] In fact, this was only one stage in a larger network of long-distance sea-based trade routes that bisected India in classical times.

CLASSICAL INDIA IN THE WORLD TRADE SYSTEM

In the early centuries CE, Tamil poets celebrated the southern port city of Muciri on the west coast in present-day Kerala.

> In Muciri with its drums, where the ocean roars,
> where the paddy traded for fish and stacked high
> on the boats makes boats and houses look the same

and the sacks of pepper rose up beside them
make the houses look the same as the tumultuous
shore and the golden wares brought by the ships
are carried to land in the servicing boats,
Kuttavan its king to whom toddy is no more
valuable than water, who wears a shining garland, gives out gifts
of goods from the mountains along with goods from the sea
to those who have come to him . . .

> (*Purananuru*, in Hart and Heifetz 2002: 195–96)

The poet here evokes a place of vigorous trade where rice is brought from inland paddy fields and pepper from the hills to trade for fish hauled in from the sea. Large ships moored near shore have brought items of gold to the port as well. The local ruler has placed himself at the center of all the exchanges of goods. In another brief vignette of Muciri, the poet identifies the great oceangoing ships as belonging to the Yavanas. He writes of

> the flourishing town of Muciri, where the large beautiful ships built by the Yavanas came with gold, disturbing the white foams of the fair Big River, called the Culli of the Ceras, and returned with pepper.
>
> (*Akananuru*, in Zvelebil 1956: 403)

The term *Yavana* here denotes Greek and Roman merchants who had crossed the Indian Ocean to trade gold for pepper and other Indian commodities.[2]

Trade routes linking India with western Asia and the Mediterranean region had existed for many centuries prior to this time, and various Indian, Arab, and Greek navigators had moved goods east and west. However, two developments provided this trade with a major boost in the period just before the common era. One was the Roman annexation of Egypt in 30 BCE. This gave the dominant power of the Mediterranean basin control over the Red Sea and direct access to ports on the west coast of the Indian Ocean. Along with this political shift there was an innovation in navigational technique. Greek and Roman skippers learned how to employ the winds of the annual monsoon to sail directly across the Indian Ocean rather than following the much lengthier and slower route that hugged the coast. Most likely the Greeks learned it from Arab or Indian sailors. The Roman geographer Strabo relates one account in which a certain Eudoxus of Cyzicus, an ambassador to Egypt, encounters a shipwrecked Indian navigator. Once the Indian learns Greek, he offers to take Eudoxus to India. Eudoxus accompanies the unnamed Indian sailor across the Indian Ocean and returns with a valuable cargo of perfumes and precious stones, which the Egyptian king immediately confiscates. This anonymous Indian navigator, Strabo suggests, was the first one to show sailors from the West how to employ the monsoon winds for long-distance trade.[3]

During the first two centuries CE this sea trade between Rome and India reached its peak.

We know of the trade not only from Roman coins and other archaeological remains in India but also from classical writers such as Strabo and Pliny the Elder and especially from an anonymous Greek work, the *Periplus Maris Erythraei* or *Sailing Guide to the Indian Ocean.* The *Periplus*, composed in the first century CE, is a kind of businessman's handbook to the Indian Ocean trade, written by an Egyptian Greek merchant who had traveled these trade routes to Africa and India himself (Casson 1989). The author gives matter-of-fact advice on routes, ports, and merchandise.

Using this text, we can follow a shipment as it made its way from the Mediterranean to the southern coast of India and retrace the cargo that came back from India. A shipment might begin at Alexandria, the great Egyptian port where goods arrived from every part of the Mediterranean. From Alexandria the cargo would be transported up the Nile River to a river port, Coptos, where the Nile comes closest to the Red Sea. From there it would be taken overland through the desert, by camel, to a seaport on the Red Sea, usually Myos Hormos or Berenice. Next the goods were loaded onto large, seaworthy sailing vessels and transported south around the southern tip of the Arabian Peninsula into the Gulf of Aden. The *Periplus* describes three main routes a ship might take from there: along the eastern coast of Africa, along the Arabian coast, or (employing the monsoon winds) straight across the Indian Ocean to the western coast of the Indian subcontinent. There it could anchor at principal ports such as Barygaza (Bharukaccha, modern Bharuch) on the Gulf of Cambay in present-day Gujarat, Kalligeris (Kanhagiri) along the Maharashtra coast near present-day Mumbai, or in the south at Muziris (Muciri) in modern Kerala near the city of Kochi (see map 1.1). It took large sturdy vessels to survive the gale-force winds of the monsoon for the direct ocean route, but the rewards in time saved made it well worthwhile.

Much of the trade was in luxury items. Elites in the Roman Empire acquired from India spices such as pepper grown in the mountainous areas of the Western Ghats and ornamental items such as pearls, diamonds, and tortoiseshell. Ivory from the tusks of Indian elephants was a prized material; an Indian ivory ornament was found in the ruins of Pompeii, buried there when Vesuvius erupted in 79 CE. Exotic Indian animals such as tigers and leopards were transported as well, for the amusement and amazement of Roman audiences. And two types of textiles from Asia elicited tremendous demand in the Mediterranean world. Fine cotton cloth, from a plant first domesticated centuries earlier in South Asia, was a wondrous novelty for Roman wearers.

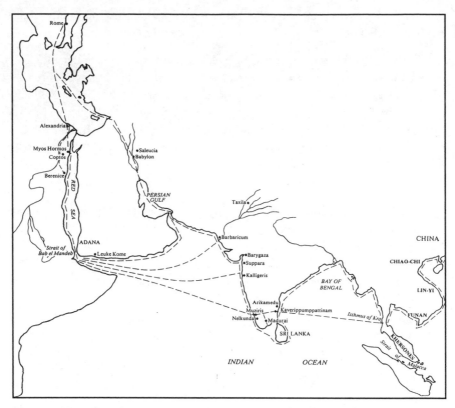

Map. 1.1: Major First-Century Maritime Routes. Reprinted from Kenneth Hall, *Maritime Trade and State Development in Early Southeast Asia* (1985). Reproduced courtesy of the University of Hawai'i Press.

The Greek historian Herodotus had already reported this fabulous product of India a few centuries earlier, writing, "There are wild trees there which produce a kind of wool which is more attractive and of a better quality than sheep's wool" (Waterfield 1998: 213). By classical times, Indians in the cotton industry had mastered the arts of weaving and colorfast dyeing and exported large amounts of this remarkable commodity.[4] The second prized textile was Chinese silk, much of which was channeled through the Indian Ocean route on its way to the Mediterranean. We will return to the Chinese and their silk in a later chapter.

Trade is always a two-way transaction. Compared to the large Roman demand for commodities from the East, Rome did not have a great deal to offer that Indians wanted. Roman merchants did bring drugs, cosmetics, silverware, and glassware, which found a market in southern India. For rulers and their courts, they brought fine ointments, wine, and trained slaves both male and female. The incorporation of a Roman Mediterranean style of luxury

10

into South Indian court life was celebrated in a Tamil poem of the second century by Nakkiranan, in his praise of the ruler of Madurai.

> May you live on, with a sweet life,
> giving away precious ornaments to all those who come to you in need
> and never running out of them, while every day you take your pleasure
>   as women
> wearing their shining bangles bring you the cool and fragrant wine
> carried here in their excellent ships by the Greeks and the women pour it
> for you out of pitchers made of gold that have been fashioned with high
> artistry, O Maran . . .
>
> (*Purananuru* 56, in Hart and Heifetz 2002: 43)

The greatest demand in India was for gold, which was used to fashion ornaments, bangles, pitchers, and other objects of luxury. The author of the *Periplus* recommended that merchants going to India should have a large supply of gold coins. The insatiable Indian appetite for gold, however, led to a cash flow problem for Rome in its overseas trade, as classical authors lamented. Writing in the mid–first century, Pliny the Elder observed that India was absorbing fifty-five million gold coins from Rome every year. This also helps us understand why a high school art teacher could still find Roman coins in a Madurai riverbed nineteen hundred years later.

Merchants from the Mediterranean, whom the Indians called Yavanas, established permanent trading posts along the southern Indian coast. At these port settlements they could collect commodities from the inland Indian trade for shipment abroad. Archaeologists have extensively excavated Arikamedu, one of these Yavana trade settlements along the Tamil coast, and found abundant Mediterranean imports, including Roman clay bowls, Egyptian pottery, and amphorae for wine and oil.[5] It may have been during this

Figure 1.1: Plaque with Royal Family (Chandraketugarh, India, first century BCE). Metropolitan Museum of Art. Image © Metropolitan Museum of Art, New York.

period that Jewish groups migrated from the Mediterranean to the west coast of India and set themselves up as traders.[6] However, the trade was not controlled or even dominated by Mediterranean merchants coming east; Indian traders and sailors traveled west as well, like Strabo's shipwrecked captain in Egypt. Strabo mentions that the Pandyan king of Madurai sent an embassy to the court of the Roman emperor Augustus. In the first two centuries CE merchants from the Mediterranean and India engaged in a vigorous two-way trade that introduced new commodities into each region.

The sea trade extending east from the Mediterranean did not end in India. From the southern and eastern ports of the subcontinent, other sea routes led still farther east into Southeast Asia and from there to China. From India, traders plied their goods across the Bay of Bengal to the west coast of the Malay Peninsula, portaged them across the Isthmus of Kra to the Gulf of Thailand, reloaded them on ships, and transported them along the coast to ports on the Mekong Delta of present-day Cambodia and Vietnam. Meanwhile, other trade routes brought merchandise for exchange southward from coastal China (see map 1.1). Silk passed from the looms of China through Southeast Asia to India and on to the Mediterranean to clothe the Roman elite. Spices such as cloves, nutmeg, and mace from the Molucca Islands (later known as the Spice Islands, now part of Indonesia) made their lengthy journey westward to invigorate the meals and disguise the bad breath of Romans.[7] Other items, including beads of semiprecious stones from India and gold coins from Rome, traveled eastward into Southeast Asia. In the first centuries of the common era, India became a central node in an international system of sea trade that brought together the portion of Western Europe under Roman control, the Mediterranean basin, Egypt and the Red Sea, the southern coast of Asia, coastal Southeast Asia, and South China. As I. C. Glover and other historians have observed, this was the first appearance of a "World System . . . the economic integration by trade of most of the inhabited globe" (1989: 12).

This world trade system had profound effects on Southeast Asia. During this period, the first large Southeast Asian state was established along the lower Mekong Delta. The capital of this polity was Vyadapura, in present-day Cambodia, and its main seaport was at Oc-eo, near the mouth of the Mekong River in modern Vietnam. The Chinese chronicles of the time called it Funan, probably from a Khmer word meaning "mountain." According to later traditions, the kingdom of Funan was founded when a local queen or princess (sometimes identified as a female Naga, a semidivine snake being) was defeated in battle by a Brahman merchant from India, Kaundinya. The local princess and the Indian interloper married, and their offspring established the line of Funan royalty.[8] The story points to the presence of Indian merchants in the new state and indicates an interaction between indigenous and outside social and cultural forces in the making of Funan, a "marriage of interests," as Kenneth Hall (1985) puts it. Archaeological evidence supports this narrative theme, for many Indic elements, such as Sanskrit language, Hindu and Buddhist religious imagery, and Indian models of kingship, were assimilated into the developing culture of Funan and other political states in Southeast Asia over the next several centuries.[9]

THE WAY TO THE LAND OF GOLD

Although Indian navigators and traders were key participants in this global trade network of classical times, the Indian tradition did not preserve navigational guides or merchant manuals like the *Periplus Maris Erythraei*. However, much of the flavor, the adventurous spirit and acquisitive ethos, of the lives of Indian merchants is conveyed in the abundant Indic story literature of the period. Picaresque tales of the fantastic voyages and get-rich-quick enterprises of seafaring traders appear in numerous Indian story collections, both religious and secular. Particularly interesting is a set of stories involving trading expeditions to a place identified as the City, Island, or Land of Gold (*suvarnanagara, suvarnadvipa,* and *suvarnabhumi*). This golden region always lies somewhere across the seas to the east of the Indian subcontinent. Merchants set out from large Indian port cities such as Bharukaccha on the Arabian Sea or Tamralipti on the Bay of Bengal. To reach it required a treacherous passage by boat, but this distant land also offered tantalizing possibilities of great wealth. None of the stories provide precise geographical locations for the Land of Gold, however, and this has left modern historians and geographers free to devise their own hypotheses. It might have been Sri Lanka, Burma, Thailand, Sumatra, or some other part of Southeast Asia. As Paul Wheatley observes, the precise location of the Land of Gold was not so important to the storytellers; they viewed it simply as "a beckoning eldorado beyond the ocean" (1983: 267).[10]

Many of the protagonists in these stories belong, not surprisingly, to the merchant class (*vanij*).[11] Wealthy merchants often live in palatial homes in gleaming cities filled with other mansions. But members of other social classes, including royalty and the Brahman or priestly class, also engage actively in the overseas trade. Many stories begin when the protagonists have squandered or lost their fortunes in lives of dissipation. Gambling and consorting with greedy prostitutes appear, in these tales, as the surest ways for young city-dwellers to waste their legacies. They then set out on high-risk, high-reward voyages in hopes of regaining their wealth and with it their social standing. As one merchant-hero reflects, before setting out on a trip to recover his lost wealth:

> May everyone make wealth! There is no other spear for
> defeating enemies! If one has it, it will eat even the enemy's
> life. Without a doubt, it can effect anything including happiness
> and virtue. But wealth through effort only is true wealth and none
> other.
>
> (*Civakacintamani*, in Ryan 2005: 133)

They recognize the dangers of the trip. One mother anxiously but unsuccessfully tries to dissuade her son, Polajanaka, from a sea voyage to the Land of Gold, pleading, "My son, the sea has few chances of success and many dangers—do not go." (Cowell 1957.6: 22)

Polajanaka's mother is correct; the ocean is a formidable obstacle. The stories of the Land of Gold regularly involve difficulties at sea. Some result from natural causes. Ships are sometimes stuck in the doldrums, while at other times they are blown off course by gale-force winds. The wooden vessels may spring leaks or be blown apart by storms. In other stories the sea holds more exotic dangers. Whales or other immense sea creatures may break or swallow ships. In one Jain story, a trading fleet of five hundred ships falls into a kind of gigantic whirlpool, described as "the hollow of a snake-encircled mountain." In another Buddhist story a trading ship wanders off course and finally arrives at an immense waterfall where the ocean seems to fall into the abyss. According to the ship's captain, they have reached the Mouth of the Mare (*vadavan-mukha*), the entry to the abode of Death. Luckily the captain, who is the future Buddha, is able to steer the ship away from this brink at the end of the world.

Many ships and sailors are destroyed en route to the Land of Gold. In one Buddhist story we hear of a seaside town inhabited by female goblins (Yakshis) who trick shipwrecked sailors into marriage and then devour them. But the storytellers are more concerned with those who survive. Shipwrecked merchants cling to life by treading water, holding onto wooden pieces of the wreckage, or swimming for up to seven days. In one story the protagonist is swallowed by a whale, and emerges alive when fishermen catch the whale and cut it open. Sometimes more dramatic strategies are required. When the five hundred ships are swirling around in the mountain hollow, the ship's captain explains that a volunteer is required to perform a daring act. The protagonist, Nagadatta, climbs to the top of the mountain and sounds a gong there, which causes a flock of giant *bharanda* birds to take flight. The powerful wind from the flapping wings of these great birds dislodges the ships from the mountain hollow and saves the fleet.

Figure 1.2: Frieze with Naga and Sea Monster (Sonkh, India, first century CE). *Source:* Image © AAAUM - ACSAA #2849.

The sea is a place of danger, but it is also the realm of the fantastic. In several Buddhist *jataka* tales the goddess Manimekhala, guardian of the sea, intervenes to save virtuous shipwrecked sailors. Another Buddhist story tells of Mittavindaka, whom bad luck seems to follow. When the ship he is on comes to a standstill in midocean, the crew elects to throw him overboard. The ship then goes on its way toward the Land of Gold. Meanwhile, Mittavindaka encounters four goddesses who dwell in crystal palaces in the middle of the ocean. In another tale from the secular *Ocean of Story*, a Brahman minister returning from the Island of Gold sees a great wishing tree rise up from an ocean wave. The branches of the tree glitter with gold, its twigs are coral, and its fruits and flowers are jewels. At its trunk lies a beautiful young maiden, who plays a stringed vina and sings him a lovely song, then plunges back into the ocean. The Brahman believes he must have seen a hallucination, but the ship's captain and crew assure him that this woman, who is a semidivine Vidyadhari, always appears at the same place in the midst of the ocean singing the same song. When the minister returns to the capital and tells his king of the vision, the king becomes obsessed with finding the maiden. He leaves his kingdom, disguises himself as an ascetic, puts out to sea toward the Island of Gold, sees the same woman and hears the same song, and precipitously jumps into the ocean. But the king's dangerous quest has a happy outcome. He finds a splendid city under the sea, locates the beguiling Vidyadhari woman, and (to make a long story short) marries her and brings her back to his own capital as queen.

The stories generally devote more attention to the journey than the Land of Gold itself. The destination is often portrayed simply as a place of "buying and selling." The mechanics of trade evidently do not make for exciting tales of adventure. But when the merchant Citattan reaches the Island of Gold he enjoys himself for some time with the beautiful women of the island before trading his commodities and returning to the mainland. In some stories the

Land of Gold is portrayed as the home of other categories of beings altogether such as semidivine Vidyadharas. Difficult of access, it is a place of Otherness, both dangerous and attractive. It is a common narrative practice in the story literature of India to transform cultural and social outsiders into supernatural beings. We will see a similar allegorical treatment in the epic *Ramayana*.

The Land of Gold, it should be added, also appears in Buddhist accounts of the spread of the Buddha's teachings or dharma. Buddhist missionaries travel there to convert the local population. According to the Sri Lankan chronicle *Mahavamsa*, Sona and Uttara, two Buddhist elders sent to the Land of Gold, first must rescue the local rulers from terrible demons (*rakkhasa*, Sanskrit *raksasa*) who were eating all the royal offspring. The Buddhist missionaries succeed by creating a larger army of demons to chase away the prince-eating ones and then convert the nobility with their preaching. The Land of Gold is made safe, in this story, for the spread of the Buddhist faith. We will return to the global role of Buddhist missionaries in the next chapter.

As difficult as the route across the seas to the Land of Gold may be, the rewards for the brave, resourceful, and virtuous merchants who survive the journey are great. They gain great wealth. And wealth is often tied to other important acquisitions. Male adventurers gain beautiful females (and sometimes superhuman ones) as wives. Merchant sons who have lost their inheritance during a dissolute youth can regain their honor and place in society through a successful trading expedition to the Land of Gold. The stories of the Land of Gold were fictional tales, of course, but collectively they reveal a great deal about the mentalities of those Indians of the classical period who did engage in the risky, lucrative overseas trade.

The long-distance sea trade that linked coastal India to a vast intercontinental network stretching from the Roman to the Chinese empires and the adventurous sea expeditions of Indian merchants to the Land of Gold are only one part of the global trade in classical times. Another overland trade network that developed during the same period also had Rome and China as its endpoints. This has come to be known as the Silk Road since Chinese silk was originally one of its prime trade commodities. India played a significant intermediary role in the early development of this route as well. We will explore this further in chapter 3, focusing on the northern Indian empire of the Kushanas and their promotion of Asian trade.

2

MISSIONARIES

Modern visitors to the ancient town of Bodhgaya, in the northern Indian state of Bihar, might wonder if they have wandered by mistake into some other country. One encounters a large Tibetan monastery, which houses a substantial community of vermillion-robed Tibetan monks. Another monastery and temple nearby are Chinese in style, while farther along stands a Japanese temple, which closely resembles the wooden temples of Horyuji. A Thai monastery is modeled on a prototype in Bangkok, and a Burmese temple emulates the ancient ones of Pagan. There are structures in the local styles of Bhutan, Nepal, and Vietnam. And one cannot miss the giant seated Buddha, looming sixty-four feet high, watching over the entire multicultural assembly. Seven years in the making, this immense meditative figure was sponsored by a Japanese Buddhist sect and consecrated by the Tibetan Buddhist leader, the Dalai Lama, in November 1989 with the aim to "spread the Buddha's rays over the whole world" (see figure 2.1). The old pilgrimage town has become a living museum of Asian religious architecture and a meeting place for Buddhists from around the world.

Figure 2.1: Monolithic Buddha at Bodh Gaya (modern construction, 1989). Photograph by the author.

BUDDHISM AS A MISSIONARY RELIGION

It is no accident that Bodhgaya should have become a pan-Asian religious center. It was here, in 521 BCE, that the thirty-five-year-old Gautama Siddhartha sat down under a ficus tree, immersed himself in deep meditation, gained enlightenment, and thus became the Buddha, the "awakened one." For centuries the place of enlightenment has been a holy site for those who follow his teachings. And his message from the start was expansive and universalistic.

Followers of the Buddha were not the only traveling preachers in South Asia during the early centuries CE. Many Hindu groups had their own expansive agendas, as we will see in chapter 4. Itinerant Jain teachers circulated through the subcontinent spreading the teachings of their main founder, Mahavira. And during this period advocates of a new religious community from the Mediterranean, followers of Jesus, arrived in southern India with their own message of salvation. According to strongly-held local tradition, the first Christian church in India was established by the apostle Thomas, who landed on the Malabar coast in 52 CE.[1] The Thomas Christian church, however, remained a small, local religious community in South Asia for many centuries. In this chapter, we will focus on the most dynamic and successful missionary movement in the Asian world during the classical period—Buddhism.

The earliest Buddhist texts narrate how the Buddha himself promoted this missionary agenda among his followers. According to the *Mahavagga*'s account of his early career, after his enlightenment the Buddha initially harbored doubts about preaching. Wouldn't his discoveries prove too subtle and difficult for other humans to comprehend, immersed as they were in a world of desire and ignorance? With a little prompting from the god Brahman, though, the Buddha made the decision to teach and seek ways to deliver his message most effectively to varied audiences. Once he chose a life of teaching others, he pursued it diligently for the remaining forty-five years of his life, traveling throughout the Gangetic Plain of northern India. The *Mahavagga*, a portion of the Pali *Vinaya* (Book of Discipline) of the Theravada school, goes on to narrate the beginnings of the Buddhist mission. Soon after his enlightenment the Buddha converted Yasa, the son of a wealthy urban merchant in Varanasi, along with a large group of Yasa's friends. As soon as he had gathered sixty disciples, the Buddha sent them out to spread the teaching:

> Go ye now, O Bhikkhus, and wander for the gain of the many, out of compassion for the world, for the good, for the gain, and for the welfare of gods and men. Let not two of you go the same way. Preach, O Bhikkhus,

the doctrine which is glorious in the beginning, glorious in the middle, glorious in the end, in the spirit and in the letter; proclaim a consummate, perfect, and pure life of holiness. There are beings whose mental eyes are covered by scarcely any dust, but if the doctrine is not preached to them, they cannot attain salvation. They will understand the doctrine.

(*Mahavagga* 11.1, in Rhys Davids and Oldenberg 1881: 1.112–13)

The Buddha's followers are dispatched with the conviction that they carry a set of teachings beneficial for all and unique in its capacity to grant religious salvation.

This emphasis on a universal message and the need to extend it to all helped make the Buddhist Sangha a dynamic cosmopolitan religious community that spread throughout Asia in the ensuing centuries. Starting in the third century BCE, Indian rulers participated and aided in Buddhist proselytizing. In 262 BCE the Mauryan emperor Ashoka became a lay follower and active patron of the Buddhist Order or Sangha. In his inscriptions Ashoka explains that the great remorse he felt after a particularly bloody battle fought to subdue the region of Kalinga (modern Orissa) led him to make a personal commitment to Buddhist teachings. He visited the important places in the life of the Buddha, including Bodhgaya, and made lavish donations at these pilgrimage sites (see figure 2.2). He promoted the activities of the Buddhist

Figure 2.2: Ashoka's visit to Bodhi Tree in Bodh Gaya (Stupa Gateway, Sanchi, India, first century CE). Image © AAAUM - ACSAA #3012. Photograph courtesy of Wendy Holden.

monks and nuns and even sought to advise them on which texts they should study. In 247 BCE he convened a great council of the Buddhist Sangha in his capital, led by the eminent elder monk Moggaliputta Tissa and attended by a thousand monks. As ruler of a large empire that controlled most of the Indian subcontinent, as well as parts of Central Asia, Ashoka no doubt saw in the universalist ethics of the Buddha's teachings a powerful means of uniting peoples of diverse cultures and ethnicities into a single polity. Through his active engagement in Buddhist affairs, Ashoka came to be seen as a second "turner of the wheel" of Buddhist dharma and set an example for later rulers to emulate both in India and beyond (Reynolds 1972).

After the council, Moggaliputta Tissa sent out preachers to neighboring lands. As the Sri Lankan Buddhist chronicle *Mahavamsa* relates, he dispatched Buddhist elders from northern India to Kashmir and Gandhara, Mahasamandala (the Narmada River valley), Vanavasa (northern Karnataka), Aparantaka (the west coast of Gujarat and Maharashtra), central Maharashtra, Yonaloka (Kerala), the Himalayan foothills, the Land of Gold, and Sri Lanka (*Mahavamsa* 12.1–6). It is important to note that most of these territories, then regarded as borderlands (*paccanta*), now form part of the nation-state of India. There was no preexisting political or cultural entity that corresponded to modern India, and during this period much of the South Asian peninsula was just as "foreign" to the inhabitants of northern India as were Rome, Persia, or China. What was important to Moggaliputta was to extend the borders of the Buddha's teachings, much as the Buddha himself had sought.

This was not always a simple or peaceful matter. The *Mahavamsa* relates how in Kashmir a ruler of the Nagas (semidivine snake beings) opposed the arrival of the Buddhist teachers by causing all sorts of meteorological calamities: "Great winds blew, clouds rained and thundered, thunderbolts crashed and lightning flashed, trees and the peaks of mountains were hurled down." The Naga king himself spits smoke and fire. The Buddhist monks are unperturbed by all this hostility, however, and finally succeed in subduing and converting the king and his retinue. The king even invites the chief Buddhist monk to sit on his own royal throne and fans him like an attendant. We have already seen the similar account of Sona and Uttara counteracting the demons in the Land of Gold. Legends like these recognize that the dissemination of the Buddhist religious message into new territories did not go unopposed, but the *Mahavamsa* (being a Buddhist text) celebrates the eventual success of the Buddhist missionary enterprise.

Despite Ashoka's efforts at consolidation, the Mauryan empire survived only fifty years after his death. However, the example he established of Buddhist imperial sovereignty did persist, and the impetus he gave to the spread of the Buddhist Sangha continued. From the second century BCE to the first century CE, Buddhism became a powerful religious force in virtually all of India, the Indo-Greek regions to the northwest of the subcontinent, Central Asia, and Sri Lanka (Reynolds and Hallisey 1987). This dynamic growth in the order resulted from the travels and missionizing activities of Buddhist monks and nuns, as depicted in texts such as the *Mahavagga* and *Mahavamsa*, and from the adoption of Buddhism as a unifying ideology or imperial-level religion, following the model of Ashoka, by ambitious rulers and polities seeking to extend and secure control over culturally diverse territories.

During the second century BCE, two prominent examples of the imperial adoption of Buddhism beyond the Indian subcontinent are the rulers Duttagamini in Sri Lanka and the Indo-Greek Menander in the Bactria region of modern Afghanistan. Duttagamini (r. 161–137 BCE) began as a chieftain of a minor Sinhala kingdom and succeeded through a series of military campaigns in bringing the entire island of Sri Lanka under a single ruler for the first time. Like Ashoka, he became a great royal patron of Buddhist institutions, including the construction of the Great Stupa at Anuradhapura, and even ceremonially presented his sovereignty itself to the Buddha's relics. The narrative of Duttagamini's career and his exemplary support for the Buddhist Order in Sri Lanka recorded in the *Mahavamsa* became a powerful model for subsequent rulers in Sri Lanka and Southeast Asia.[2]

Duttagamini's contemporary far to the northwest, Menander (r. 160–135 BCE) was born in the Caucasus area and rose to rule in the region of Bactria. This area had been part of Alexander the Great's conquests in the fourth century BCE, and it retained a Hellenistic culture under the Seleucids. Indian texts refer to Menander as a Yavana, pointing to his Greek background. Through a vigorous series of campaigns, Menander carved out an extensive kingdom that reached from the Kabul Valley in the west to the Ravi River in the east, comprising much of modern-day Afghanistan and Pakistan. He led raids into Rajasthan and eastward into the Ganges River valley as far as Pataliputra, the former Mauryan capital. Like Duttagamini, Menander adopted Buddhism as the ruling ideology of his new realm. Buddhist tradition attributes the conversion of this Indo-Greek king to the lengthy intellectual arguments of a Buddhist elder, Nagasena, as recorded in the *Milindapanha* (Questions of King Menander). This text, found in the collections of several schools, is a Buddhist apologetic work, possibly modeled on the dialogues of Plato, aimed at Greek and Eurasian audiences.[3] However, Menander's adoption of Buddhist imagery and ideology likely also involved strategic considerations in his effort to unite the diverse territories he had conquered.

During the period of the first two centuries CE, three major developments contributed to the global Buddhist mission. The first was the establishment or consolidation of overland trade routes, later known as the Silk Road, stretching from Han China westward across Central Asia toward the Roman-ruled Mediterranean. The second was the organization of the Kushana empire, initially based in the Kabul region and later reaching from Central Asia into the Gangetic Plain of northern India. The third was the beginning of Buddhist missionary activity in China. Although they are closely interrelated, we will deal with the third of these events in this chapter and return to the Kushanas and the Silk Road in chapter 3.

BUDDHISM BECOMES A CHINESE RELIGION

The introduction of Buddhism into China, according to one well-known story, began with a dream. One night the Chinese emperor Ming (r. 57–75 CE) saw a golden deity flying around in front of the imperial palace. The next morning, he inquired among his ministers to see if any could explain this extraordinary apparition. One minister reported that he had heard of a sage in India who had attained salvation. The body of this sage was said to have a golden hue, and he could fly. The minister added that this sage was known there as the Buddha. The emperor immediately dispatched a group of envoys to find out about the remarkable sage and his teachings. The envoys later returned from India with teachings of the Buddha, with relics and holy images, and in some versions with two Indian Buddhist monks, Dharmaraksa and Matanga (Ch'en 1964: 29–30).

Whatever the veracity of this legend, the earliest clear historical record of a Buddhist presence in China does date to the reign of Emperor Ming. In 65 CE, Prince Ying, half brother to the emperor, sponsored a sumptuous vegetarian feast for the pious monks and laymen in P'eng-ch'eng, a commercial center in northern Kiangsu. In the first century CE, evidently, Buddhist communities sprang up in several places in China, including western outposts such as Dunhuang and the capital at Lo-yang. The advent of Buddhism in China must be linked, in a broader sense, to several developments. First, the consolidation and westward expansion of the Chinese empire under the Han dynasty brought Chinese rulers into contact with cultures to the west. Central Asian states such as Bactria, Parthia, and Scythia sent diplomatic missions to the Chinese capital, and Buddhist monks probably accompanied these missions. The westward expansion of China also facilitated the overland caravan trade through Central Asia into South Asia, and itinerant Buddhist monks traveled together with sympathetic merchants along these new trade routes to find new patrons and spread their message. By dream, diplomacy, or caravan, however they arrived, Buddhist teachers and their teachings gained a significant foothold in China in the first two centuries CE.

The process of turning Buddhism into a Chinese religion, however, involved a complex interaction between differing cultures. Missionaries, as the Buddha himself acknowledged, must adapt their message to new audiences. By the first century CE, Buddhists in India had created an enormous, diverse, and often abstruse corpus of texts. There were multiple schools of Buddhist thought, each with its own distinctive doctrines. Moreover, Indian Buddhism was inextricably tied to other Indic disciplines of knowledge. China, of course, already had its own intellectual disciplines and its own Confucian and Taoist religious traditions. The primary task of the early Buddhists in China was to find a way to translate Indian Buddhist thought in a way that would be comprehensible to a Chinese audience. The outcome, as Stephen Teiser observes (2005: 1160), was a "hybrid" involving both Indian and Chinese contributions in the creation of something distinct and new. The first Buddhists in China were immigrants from the Kushana-ruled areas of Northwest India and from smaller Central Asian kingdoms. They brought with them texts, either memorized or handwritten in manuscript form, that had been composed in the Indian languages of Sanskrit or its Prakrit derivatives. When they arrived in China, they did not speak Chinese. To translate their Buddhist texts or explain their ideas, they had to find Chinese collaborators. The Chinese speakers in turn had to find ways to express the unfamiliar Buddhist concepts in familiar Chinese terminology. Translation became a committee affair in which no one understood both the Indian and Chinese languages sufficiently to judge the result.

The most successful early Buddhist translator was An Shih-kao, a monk from a royal family of Parthia (in the modern area of northern Iran and Afghanistan). After renouncing his succession to the Parthian throne, he studied in a Buddhist monastery and then traveled to the Chinese capital of Lo-yang in 148 CE during the reign of Emperor Han. With the support of pious lay followers, he established a translation center there with An-hsuan, a trader from Parthia who had become a Buddhist evangelist, and a Chinese convert, Yen Fou-t'iao. Working together, one member of the team would recite or read the Indic original aloud, another bilingual member would suggest a Chinese translational equivalent, and an assistant would note it down in writing. Others would be employed to check for accuracy. Sometimes the Parthian master would add some oral explication to the text, and this might be incorporated into the new translation. Then a Chinese collaborator would polish the style, and the monks would ascertain if the final translation was true to the original source. An Shih-kao's team, focusing especially on texts concerning Buddhist meditative techniques, translated somewhere between thirty-five and ninety works, according to later listings, and also established a collaborative translational method that would be employed by many later Buddhists in China (Ch'en 1965: 43; Zürcher 1972: 31).

Even with this conscientious working method, questions of cultural translation emerged. Was it possible for key Buddhist terms to be given Chinese equivalents? For example, the important Indic term *dharma* was rendered by the Chinese term *fa* (law, principle, method), which conveyed its own penumbra of meaning. In some cases, new Chinese words had to be created. *Buddha* became *Fotuo* in Chinese, an attempt simply to mimic in Chinese the sound of the Sanskrit. In a broader sense, Indian concepts also had to be rendered in ways at least somewhat familiar within Chinese culture. The Indian notion of *karma*, with its connotations of moral retribution and transmigration, found an imperfect analogy in the Chinese ideas of one's individual lot (*fen*) and destiny (*ming*). The practice of renouncing a worldly life, so fundamental to Buddhist monasticism, could be understood as more or less parallel to the Chinese ideal of the wise sage who retires from public affairs. Buddhist techniques of meditation had at least a few similarities with existing Taoist practices of breath control and trance (Teiser 2005: 1160; Gernet 1996: 215). These processes of encounter, comparison, competition, and dialogue between Indian Buddhist ideas and practices and those already present in China would lead over time to innovative understandings and developments both within Buddhism and beyond it.

The introduction of Buddhism from South Asia into China did not pass unnoticed, and it is not surprising that partisans of other religious practices would raise vehement objections. Confucians, in particular, argued that the Buddhist promotion of renunciation violated the central value of *xiao* (filial piety). They viewed the Buddhist goal of individual nirvana to be selfish and antisocial. One anti-Buddhist polemic from this period was the *T'ai-p'ing-ching* (Sutra of the Great Peace), written from a Taoist perspective probably in the second century (Ch'en 1965: 51–52). Like the Confucians, the Taoist author of this work accused Buddhists of encouraging people to abandon parents, wives, and children. Buddhism promoted the undignified practice of begging, this text asserted, and it encouraged the ingestion of impurities, namely, drinking urine as a form of medicine. Relations between the early Buddhists in China and indigenous Taoists were not all antagonistic, however, and other observers pointed to the similarities between the two disciplines. Some Taoists found in the Buddhist practices of meditation a technique well suited to their own religious aims. Some even suggested that Lao-tzu, the mystic founder of Taoism, had originally traveled west, reached India, and converted the Buddhists. The intricate relations between the Buddhists in China and the Confucian and Taoist establishments over the ensuing centuries, with all their conflicts and accommodations, is a fascinating topic in the history of religions, but it is beyond the scope of this booklet.[4]

From its initial advent in China in the first two centuries CE, Buddhism would become in later centuries a fully Chinese religion with many different schools and sects. Modern scholars have characterized the complex encounter between a religious formation originating in India and the indigenous Chinese culture in various ways. At one pole, the "Buddhist conquest of China" (as the title of Eric Zürcher's study puts it) suggests the warriorlike agency of Buddhist ideas in a new social environment. By contrast, the "sinification" of Buddhism, as others describe the encounter, stresses the ways Buddhism was altered and assimilated in its new setting. Chinese Buddhism as a "hybrid," adopting a genetic analogy, points to the more or less equal contributions of two sources, Indic Buddhism and Chinese culture, resulting in a new crossbreed, Chinese Buddhism. From the "global India" perspective of this booklet, the entry of Buddhism into China can be seen as a step in the global mission set in motion by the Buddha and pursued vigorously by his followers and as another way in which, through the actions of these Buddhist missionaries, Indians were engaged in the cultural world system of classical times. And, it is important to remember, this "hybridization" did not occur just one time, for contacts and dialogues among Buddhists in India and China continued over many centuries.

BUDDHIST EXCHANGES: TRANSLATORS AND PILGRIMS

The beginnings of intellectual and cultural contacts between India and China in the early centuries CE, instigated by Buddhist missionary activity, set in motion exchanges between the two areas that continued throughout the first millennium. A great religious tradition like Buddhism, however, did not travel in intellectual isolation. Since Buddhism had grown up as an inextricable part of a broader Indian culture, the importation of Buddhist learning from India into China also entailed the transmission of many other Indian disciplines of knowledge that we would consider nonreligious or secular such as mathematics, astronomy, architecture, medicine, music, and linguistics (Sen 2005: 161–90).

To illustrate the complex circulations of persons and ideas between India and China, with Central Asia often acting as mediator, initiated by the Buddhist mission, let us look briefly at the lives of two exemplary figures of the late fourth and early fifth centuries CE, the translator Kumarajiva (343–413) and the pilgrim Faxian (ca. 337–422). While this takes us a bit beyond the time period of this booklet, these two lives convey the cosmopolitan world of Asian Buddhism that had come to fruition. This was a time when Buddhism was still a powerful religious force in India, active throughout the Central Asian trading towns of the Silk Road, spreading within Southeast Asia, and emerging as a potent religious formation in China.

Kumarajiva was born in the city of Kucha, a trade center along the northern trade route in Central Asia. His father was a Brahman immigrant from India and his mother a member of the Kuchean royal family. When Kumarajiva was seven, his mother renounced her place in society to become a Buddhist nun, and Kumarajiva went along with her to become a novice. When he was nine, the two traveled to Kashmir, and the young novice had the opportunity to study with an Indian master, Bandhudatta. From Kashmir they journeyed to Kashgar, another important Central Asian city-state on the Silk Road (now in the westernmost Sinkiang region of China). Here the pupil continued his course of Buddhist studies and also studied the most ancient Hindu scriptures, the Vedas, as well as related Indic disciplines of grammar, logic, medicine, and metaphysics. It was in Kashgar that Kumarajiva met Suryasoma, a master of the newer Mahayana trends, and he became a confirmed advocate of the "Greater Vehicle" teachings. Returning finally to Kucha, Kumarajiva received his full ordination in the royal palace at age twenty and continued to study Buddhist texts with a master from North India. He also invited his old teacher Bandhudatta to emigrate from Kashmir to Kucha and managed to convert him to the new Mahayana doctrine of *sunyata* (emptiness).

By the year 379, Kumarajiva had come to be recognized throughout China as an accomplished and erudite Buddhist scholar. The Chinese ruler Fu Chien tried to bring Kumarajiva to the capital at Ch'ang-an, but instead the monk was captured by General Lu Kuang, who had been sent to bring the Kucha region under Chinese rule. Lu Kuang was evidently hostile to Buddhism, and he kept Kumarajiva under house arrest in Liang-chou (Northwest China) for seventeen years. Finally, in 401, the Chinese emperor Yao Hsing, who had succeeded Fu Chien, sent an army to defeat Lu Kuang and had Kumarajiva brought with all due honor to the capital.

In Ch'ang-an the emperor presented Kumarajiva with a garden retreat and gave him the necessary support to establish a new translation workshop. Kumarajiva was perhaps the first major Buddhist translator to be equally fluent in both the original Buddhist languages of India, such as Sanskrit, and the target language of Chinese. The now famous monk recruited assistants and set to work. It is said that a thousand monks participated in the daily sessions and that the ruler Yao Hsing also sometimes took part. Kumarajiva was given the title *kuo-shih* (national preceptor). Working from 402 until this death in 413, Kumarajiva and his team produced thirty-five important works of translation. His special interest was the Mahayana philosophical teachings of Madhyamika, and his efforts led to the formation of a new school of Chinese Mahayana known as San-lun, the School of Three Treatises (Ch'en 1965: 81–84; Todaro 1987).

About the time Kumarajiva was prevented from reaching Chang-an, a Chinese monk named Faxian (also rendered as Fa-Hsien) was planning his own expedition out of the Chinese capital. Kumarajiva's itinerary had taken him from Central Asia to India and then to China and would eventually land him in Ch'ang-an. Faxian's plan was to make a great journey from Ch'ang-an through Central Asia to India and back again. He was "distressed by the imperfect state of the Buddhist 'Disciplines' (*Vinaya*)" in China, as he explains in his later account of the journey, the *Fo-kuo-chi* (Record of the Buddhist Countries), and so he decided to travel to India, the original home of Buddhism, to acquire more complete copies of the *Vinaya* texts (Giles 1956: 1). He set out with four other Buddhist monks in 399. Two years later, as we know, Kumarajiva was brought to the capital by the emperor, and one of the texts he would translate was the *Vinaya* of the Sarvastivada school.

Figure 2.3: Statue of Kumarajiva at Kizlin Grotto, Xinjiang. *Source:* iStockphoto.com

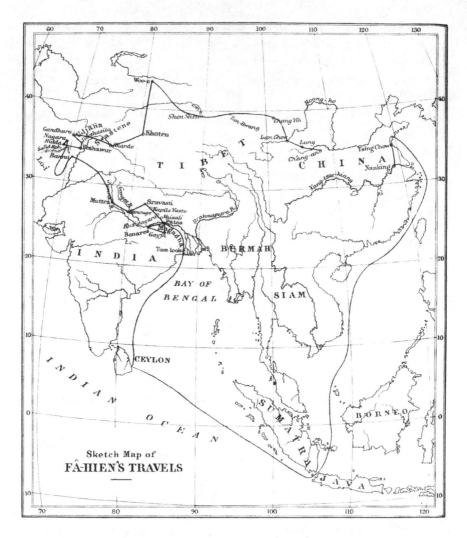

Map 2.1: The Travels of Fa-Hsien. Reprinted from H. A. Giles, *The Travels of Fa-hsien*, 1956.

Faxian and his small party traveled west through Dunhuang, Khotan, and Kashgar and then headed south across the Himalayas to the Gandhara region (see map 2.1). Faxian describes the difficulties of the route through the mountains: "On these mountains there is snow in winter and summer alike. There are also venomous dragons which, if provoked, spit forth poisonous winds, rain, snow, sand, and stones. Of those who encounter these dangers not one in ten thousand escape" (Giles 1956: 8–9). It took them three years to go from the Chinese capital through this treacherous area to northwestern India. After resting several months at Purushapura (modern Peshawar), three of the monks decided to return directly to China. Faxian continued south across

28

another range of Himalayan mountains, where one of his original traveling party died of exposure. Faxian tells of the despair he felt at this point, but he resolutely went on and finally made his way out of the mountains, into the Indus River plain, and then eastward into the vast Gangetic Plain of northern India. This was the birthplace of Buddhism, and Faxian eagerly visited all the places where the Buddha had lived and taught. At Bodhgaya he honored the tree under which the Buddha had attained enlightenment and noted that there were three large monasteries at the site where the monks were just as rigorous in their conduct as the Buddha's original followers had been during the founder's lifetime.

Faxian was an intrepid adventurer and a Buddhist pilgrim, but he was foremost a scholarly monk who had come to India to acquire better knowledge of the Buddhist tradition and to transmit this learning back to China. Accordingly, after visiting the important holy sites he stayed for three years at a monastery in Pataliputra, where he could study the Sanskrit language and Buddhist scriptures. Here he was able to copy the complete *Vinaya* of the Mahasanghika school and also a condensed version of the Sarvastivada *Vinaya* along with numerous other works.

In 407 Faxian began his return trip to China. Instead of hazarding another northern crossing of the Himalayas, he decided to travel along a southerly sea route. His companion Tao-cheng, last of the original party, found the Buddhist life in India much to his liking, and he decided to remain there permanently. Faxian went down the Ganges to Tamralipti, the port city on the Bay of Bengal, and stayed there for two more years, copying more texts and making sketches of Buddhist images. Then he shipped out to Sri Lanka, where he was able to acquire still more Buddhist texts to take with him. By this time, twelve years into his travels, even this intrepid monk was feeling deeply homesick.

> Fa-hsien [he says of himself] had now been many years away from his own land of Han; the people he had had to deal with were all inhabitants of strange countries; the mountains, the streams, plants and trees on which his eyes had lighted were not those of old days; moreover, those who had traveled with him were separated from him—some having remained behind in these countries, others having died. Now, beholding only his own shadow, he was constantly sad at heart; and when suddenly, by the side of this jade image, he saw a merchant make offering of a white silk fan from China, his feelings overcame him and his eyes filled with tears. (Giles 1956: 68)

Finally, in 411, he gained passage on a merchant ship heading east, but it was blown off course by a typhoon and landed at the Southeast Asian island of Java. After five months there Faxian was able to find another ship heading up the coast for Kuang-chou (Canton), China. However, this voyage was also disrupted by a violent gale, and after much drifting about, the ship eventually landed in Ch'ang-kuang, far to the north of its original destination. The sea route had proven just as hazardous as the overland route and had taken five years in all. From there Faxian journeyed back to Chien-k'ang (Nanking) and launched himself on the next part of his project, which was to translate into Chinese the Indian works he had brought back with him. In 416 he was asked to compose an account of his trip. Although Faxian was not the first Chinese Buddhist to go to India, he was the first to make the full round-trip and write about it. As a result we are able to read about his remarkable journey of adventure and Buddhist scholarship today (Ch'en 1965: 89–93; Yun-hua 1987).

The lives and travels of Kumarajiva and Faxian, as well as those of the earlier translators, between India and China point to an important aspect of the geography of Buddhism. Central Asian city-states such as Kucha and Kashgar and regions such as Parthia and Bactria had become important centers of Buddhist learning in their own right. The empire of the Kushanas, which originated in Central Asia, facilitated this growth.

3

WARRIORS

The tall stone figure has lost his head and arms, but there is no mistaking the power and determination in his pose (see figure 3.1). He stands with two pillar-like legs spread apart, and his oversized boots point outward to the left and right. He wears a patterned tunic and over that a long open coat of heavy material that reaches below his knees. His right hand rests on a long, sturdy mace pressed to the ground between his feet while his left hand grips the hilt of a broadsword. Along the lower part of his coat and tunic are inscribed his name and royal titles: "The Great King, the King of Kings, the Son of God, Kanishka."

In his current home in the Mathura Museum, King Kanishka looks like an armed horseman who has just jumped off his horse in the middle of a religious gathering and is about to assert his domination over it. Dressed in his Central Asia riding gear and holding signs of battle and sovereignty, he certainly stands out as an intruder among the naked Jain saints and barefoot Buddhas, seated in peaceful meditation, who populate much of the museum (Vogel 1930). What is Kanishka doing there?

Figure 3.1: Kushan Emperor Kanishka (Mathura, India, first century CE). *Source:* The Huntington Photographic Archive of Asian Art, Columbus, Ohio.

The warrior Kanishka was king of the Kushana dynasty, the most powerful ruler of the largest India-based empire of the first two centuries CE. However, as Kanishka's garb suggests, the Kushanas were not originally from India, nor was their imperial domain located only on the subcontinent. Kanishka's forebears migrated from the steppe lands of western China by way of Central Asia before finding their way to the subcontinent and establishing their kingdom. During Kanishka's reign, the Kushanas exercised influence over an immense area that reached from the Amu Darya (Oxus River) in the northwest to the Tarim Basin in the northeast and from the mouth of the Indus River in the southwest to the Ganges Plain in the southeast as far as the old Mauryan capital of Pataliputra (modern Patna). Centered in an area that spanned the modern nations of Afghanistan, northern Pakistan, and northern India, the Kushanas also extended their dominion over territories that now lie in Iran, Turkmenistan, Uzbekistan, Tajikistan, and western China (see map 3.1).

During this period, the two most powerful imperial states in the world were those of Rome and Han China. Situated between these two, the Kushanas were able to create their own expansive polity, which united a great variety of differing ethnic and cultural groups, exercised control over the overland trade routes across Asia, and facilitated the spread of Buddhism throughout Asia. The warrior tribe that established the Kushana empire thus played a crucial role in the global reach of India during the first two centuries CE.

MOVEMENTS OF A WARRIOR TRIBE

Writing from a modern Indian perspective, historians have often labeled the period 200 BCE to 200 CE the "age of foreign invasions." Between the Mauryan empire (321–185 BCE) and that of the Guptas (roughly 320–550 CE), many of the most potent ruling groups in the northern part of the subcontinent, such as the Indo-Greeks under Menander, originated outside the borders of modern India. And longtime residents of India did make use of terms to distinguish themselves and those they considered outsiders, which we will consider further in chapter 4. However, the modern national boundaries with which we view the world did not exist in classical times. Rather than projecting modern geographical borders onto the past, we can see this as another indication that India was not a world apart in the early centuries CE. The Kushanas undeniably came from outside the Indian subcontinent, but their travels and eventual empire illustrate well the more fluid social and political geography of classical times.

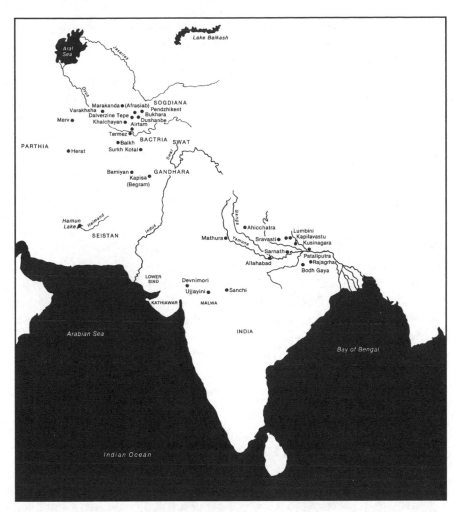

Map 3.1: India in the Kushana Period. Reprinted from Stanislaw Czuma, *Kushan Sculpture* (1985). Map by Joseph Finizia. Reproduced courtesy of the Cleveland Museum of Art.

The earliest evidence of the ethnic group that would become the Kushanas comes from northwestern China. Chinese sources refer to a large nomadic tribe known as the Yuezhi that inhabited parts of the Kansu Province. (This is the tribe that would subsequently become the Kushanas.) As the Han Chinese attempted to consolidate their rule and expand westward beginning in the second century BCE, they came into conflict with another federation of nomadic tribes, the Xiongnu. The Chinese western campaigns set off a kind of domino effect of tribes that rippled across Central Asia. The Xiongnu, pressured on their eastern flank by the Chinese, displaced the Yuezhi to the west. As the Yuezhi migrated west along the northern border of the Gobi

Desert, they pushed other groups such as the Shakas and Scythians. By the first century BCE, the Yuezhi had come to occupy the Ta-hsia region and forced the Shakas south into Bactria, the region previously ruled by the Indo-Greek king Menander. Pressured by still another nomadic group, the Yuezhi subsequently moved into the Bactrian region, which is centered on the upper Amu Darya along the northernmost border of Afghanistan, and gained control over it. As they subjugated Bactria, the Yuezhi divided their area of rule into five principalities.[1]

The beginnings of the Kushana empire came when Kujala Kadphises, the ruler of one of these principalities, the Kuei-shuang (Indianized as Kushana), set out to conquer the others and reunify the Yuezhi into a single kingdom. Once the core region of Bactria was united, Kujala undertook a series of campaigns against other regional powers, the Parthians in western Asia and the Indo-Parthians south of the Hindu Kush mountains. The Kushana expansion continued under his son and successor, Vima Kadphises. Under Vima, the Kushanas pushed eastward across the Indus River and into the Ganges Plain of northern India. After defeating the Shakas, Vima appointed a viceroy at Mathura to maintain control over these new Indian territories and returned to the northwest. He also annexed Kashmir in the northernmost part of India. In 78 CE, Kanishka ascended to the Kushana throne, and during the two and a half decades of his rule the Kushana empire reached its peak in territory and power.

The Kushana empire was not a unitary nation-state with fixed boundaries in the modern sense. Nor did it develop the stable centralized administrative structures of its contemporary empires in Rome and China. Rather, it was a large polity centered around several core regions of settled control, with extensive outlying territories of more fluctuating authority maintained through alliances with various regional chieftains or elites. The Kushanas ruled from two main centers. One was Gandhara, the well-settled region surrounding Purushapura (modern Peshawar) in northern Pakistan. Gandhara had been a cultural crossroads for several centuries, a place where Persian, Hellenistic Greek, and Indian influences collided with one another in myriad encounters. Important trade routes passed through this area, so control over Gandhara could be lucrative indeed. The second center was Mathura, a city situated on the Yamuna River in northern India. From Mathura the Kushanas sought to gain control over the fertile, wealthy, and well-populated Gangetic Plain. Purushapura and Mathura appear to have been Kushana co-capitals, and both become centers of cultural and religious innovation during Kushana times, as we will see.

Not much is known about Yuezhi culture during earliest period of their migrations. Like many peoples that originated in the vast steppe lands of Central Asia, such as the later Mongols under Genghis Khan, the Yuezhi were horsemen who followed a nomadic lifestyle and maintained a cattle-breeding, pastoral economy. Their military prowess was based on skill in horsemanship and adept use of the bow and arrow. As nomads, they traveled light and left behind only limited traces in the historical record, usually when they came to the notice of more literate record-keeping civilizations such as the Chinese or Hellenistic Greeks. For instance, the Chinese chronicle *Han-shu*, compiled about 80 CE, observes, "The Great Yueh-chih [Yuezhi] originally formed a nomadic state; they moved about, following their cattle, and had the same customs as the Hsiung-nu [Xiongnu]. As their archers numbered more than a hundred thousand, they were strong and treated the Hsiung-nu with contempt" (Zürcher 1967: 76). However, from the time of Kujala Kadphises, when they had settled down as rulers of territories, a fuller body of historical remains reveals the military and political culture the Kushanas created for themselves. They consciously maintained elements of the nomadic steppe culture from which they had come, while they also adopted and synthesized cosmopolitan influences from India, Persia, and the Greco-Roman culture of western Asia.

One good source of evidence for the cultural style of the Kushana leaders may be found in the images they had made of themselves. In these regal images, like Kanishka's immense portrait statue, the costumes consist of heavy sewn materials, quite different from the light unsown drapes of most Indian images. The figures wear pants and tunics, fastened with wide belts on the outside, and boots, the practical riding clothes of an equestrian people living in a cold climate. It appears that members of the Kushana elite retained their traditional Central Asian clothing even after they had settled in South Asia or at least wished to have themselves represented in that ancestral style. The rulers are often depicted with massive swords of a Central or West Asian type, pointing to their warrior ethos and their origin outside the subcontinent. But, significantly, in his statue Kanishka carries a large club or mace along with his sword. As John Rosenfield (1967: 179–81) notes, the mace (*danda*) fits into the existing Indic iconography of political authority and the just use of force. The Kushana rulers were referred to in inscriptions as *devaputras*, "sons of the gods." In their political ideology, then, the Kushana rulers portrayed themselves as warriors from outside India who sought to exercise royal authority according to acceptable Indian norms and enjoyed the favor of the gods in their rule.

Figure 3.2: Coin of Kanishka (Gandhara Region, Pakistan, first century CE). The Metropolitan Museum of Art, Bequest of Joseph H. Durkee. Image © Metropolitan Museum of Art, New York.

The study of coins offers another valuable window into the developing Kushana cultural style. Since coinage is largely a prerogative of the state, the coins of a kingdom like that of the Kushanas served as a "vehicle of royal propaganda, a direct expression of the ideology of the ruling house," as Rosenfield observes (1967: 70). Kujala Kadphises was the first Kushana ruler to mint coins in copper, reflecting the newfound confidence of the unified Kushana state. Vima Kadphises more ambitiously began to issue gold coins, as well as copper, and the gold issues continued under Kanishka and his successor Huvishka. It appears that the Kushanas acquired Roman gold coins through trade and then melted them down to restrike their own dynastic coins. This accounts for the scarcity of Roman coins found in northern India, in contrast to the much greater number found in the south.

What is most striking about the Kushana coins is the great breadth of imagery. Rosenfield counts thirty-three different deities that the Kushana rulers Kanishka and Huvishka chose to depict on their coins along with the figures of the human rulers. More significant, these deities derive from a number of different regions. Some, such as Herakles and Helios, clearly come from the Roman and Hellenistic world to the west. Others, such as Ahura Mazda and Mithra, originated in the Persian cultural region and were associated with the powerful Achaemenid empire of earlier centuries There were Hindu deities from India as well, including Shiva and the war god Skanda. Kanishka also issued coins depicting the Buddha. Rosenfield interprets this eclectic assembly of divine images as reflecting the Kushana rulers' "concern with material abundance and prosperity, with military triumph, with legitimacy of rule, and with the divine sanction and support of the ruling house" (1967: 70). Rulers are certainly concerned with these matters, but one can see it also as an audacious appropriation of divine figures from other kingdoms and empires throughout Asia, past and present, to forge a new, synthetic imperial order.

In this Kushana imperial order, the image of the Buddha came to play an important role on coins during the reign of Kanishka, and the Buddhism patronized by the Kushana rulers would in turn make a deep impact on the religious art of Asia.

TWO IMAGES OF THE BUDDHA

In the earliest phases of Indian Buddhist sculptural art, the Buddha himself is not shown in human form. Rather, his presence is indicated by symbols such as his footprints, a throne, an umbrella, or a tree. Art historians have long referred to this as the "aniconic" phase of Buddhist art. Sometime during the first century CE, for reasons never fully explained, sculptors began to depict the Buddha Sakyamuni in physical anthropomorphic form. The appearance of the Buddha image, then, coincides with the rise of the Kushana empire. Moreover, these images first appear, nearly simultaneously, in the two areas that form the core zones of Kushana rule, namely, Gandhara and Mathura. There is a long-standing debate about which region came first in originating the human representation of the Buddha, but this scholarly controversy need not detain us here.[2] What is more noteworthy is how the Buddha appears in these two areas.

The immense, ten-foot-tall figure known as "Bala's Buddha," now in the Sarnath Museum, stands on two firmly planted feet (see figure 3.3). From an inscription we know that the monk Bala commissioned this monumental sculpture in the third year of Kanishka's reign. It was made in Mathura and transported, no doubt by river barge, east along the Yamuna and Ganges, to Sarnath, the site of the Buddha's first sermon

Figure 3.3: Friar Bala's Buddha (Sarnath, India, first century CE). *Source:* The Huntington Photographic Archive of Asian Art, Columbus, Ohio.

(Schopen 1988: 89). The powerful figure wears a nearly transparent monastic robe draped over his left arm, which reveals his broad, rounded chest and deep navel. The face looks out with almost bulging eyes to meet the gaze of the viewer. The Buddha here projects a firm, powerful presence. His body seems to swell outward as if animated from within by a potent life breath. Yet the sculptor's treatment of the bodily form is not "realistic," in the way Western sculpture often sought to observe and reproduce the appearance of the empirical world. As the art historian A. K. Coomaraswamy put it, the sculptural artists of Mathura sought to create not the appearance, but rather the significance of their subjects (1927: 8). It is a conceptual style of religious art.

Bala's Buddha is the earliest securely dated large icon of the Buddha Sakyamuni, but sculptors in the Gandhara region were not far behind. In a typical standing Sakyamuni from the Gandhara region, such as the Standing Sakyamuni from Purushapura, now in the Cleveland Museum of Art, we can observe the same theme as in the Mathura example but with significant contrasts in the sculptural style (see figure 3.4). One might first notice the weightier treatment of the robe, which appears here more like a Greco-Roman rendering of a toga than the nearly transparent garment on Bala's Buddha. Here, Sakyamuni's eyes look downward, open but introspective, and the lines of the facial expression show greater attention to his body. If Bala's Buddha seeks

Figure 3.4: Standing Sakyamuni, Gandhara style, Pakistan, probably Takhi-i Bahi, 150–200 CE. The Cleveland Museum of Art. Gift of Morris and Eleanor Everett in memory of Flora Morris Everett, 1972.43.

to convey the powerful presence of an ideal Buddha, the Gandharan sculptor has focused more on rendering the physical beauty of a human Sakyamuni.

The contrast between these two icons gives us a sense of the broader stylistic differences between the artistic traditions as they developed in the two Kushana centers. The art of Mathura grew out of the earlier northern Indian styles associated with the Mauryan and Shunga dynasties, and the treatment of the Buddha Sakyamuni was adapted from earlier freestanding icons of Yakshas, autochthonous nature deities. The art of Gandhara, by contrast, appears to be an original synthesis. Some earlier art historians characterized Gandharan art as a provincial Greco-Roman style, but it is more accurate to see it as a conscious cosmopolitan style incorporating multiple outside influences from Hellenistic Bactria, the Roman provinces, the earlier Persians or Achaemenids, the Parthians, and India. Yet, as Lolita Nehru argues, the Gandharan artists mingled these borrowed styles with "a local Gandharan conceptual imagination, which absorbed, transformed or rejected the innumerable stylistic elements present in the Gandharan region to create an independent Gandharan stylistic language" (1989: xvii). Reflecting the ruling style of the Kushanas, the artisans of Gandhara maintained a local sensibility while at the same time synthesizing ideas and models from far afield.

The religious art and architecture of Buddhism flourished during the Kushana period, both in Mathura and in Gandhara, not only in the magnificent new standing images of Buddha Sakyamuni but also in the detailed narrative reliefs of the Buddha's life (and of his past lives, as told in the *jatakas*), and in the elaborately decorated stupas designed to serve as centers of devotional practice. The imperial reach of the Kushanas, who brought together dispersed territories into a single polity, certainly facilitated the kind of cosmopolitan style that integrated multiple traditions into a new synthesis in the Gandharan region. But it is important to ask what role the Kushana warriors and rulers played in this Buddhist efflorescence.

There is no sign that the earliest Kushana rulers had any personal inclination toward Buddhism. However, Kanishka appears to have been a great patron of Buddhist institutions. Not only did he begin to include the Buddha among the pantheon of figures on Kushana coinage, but he also patronized a major stupa and monastery in the Gandharan capital of Purushapura. Later Chinese travelers spoke of Kanishka's stupa as the grandest monument in India. "Of all pagodas and temples seen by the pilgrims," Faxian says, referring to himself, "not one could compare with this in grandeur and dignity . . . Tradition says that of the various pagodas in the inhabited world this one takes the highest rank" (Giles 1956:13). Moreover, Kanishka is supposed to have convened the fourth great Buddhist council, held in Kashmir or Gandhara, with the scholar Vasumitra presiding. He is also associated as a patron with the great poet Ashvaghosha, author of the Sanskrit classics *Buddhacarita* and *Saundarananda*.

Later Buddhist tradition came to portray Kanishka as a "second Ashoka." This is only partly true. There is no evidence that Kanishka shared Ashoka's intense personal commitment to Buddhist ethical principles, but he did emulate Ashoka's model of patronizing Buddhist institutions as part of a cosmopolitan imperial strategy of rule. No doubt Kanishka and the Kushana elites saw a political advantage in the universalizing ethics of Buddhism in their efforts to bring cohesion to the far-flung and highly diverse territories under their dominion. They had an economic interest in pan-Asian trade, and the merchants involved in this trade were often well-disposed toward Buddhism. However, any embrace of Buddhism by the Kushana court did not come at the cost of exclusion of other traditions. It did not prevent, for example, the promulgation of Hindu traditions within the empire. Kushana coins continued to depict male Hindu deities, especially one figure usually identified as Shiva. Some of the earliest recognizable images of Hindu deities—Vishnu, Shiva, Skanda, Durga, and others—appear during this period, especially in the Mathura area. In the art of Gandhara, figures from the Greco-Roman pantheon appear just as often.

Finally, Kushana patronage of Buddhist arts should be seen in light of a broader policy toward disciplines of knowledge generally. As Rosenfield points out, within the Kushana empire there lived "astronomers, mathematicians, theologians, playwrights, poets, grammarians, logicians, and physicians" (2006: 10). And, thanks to the auspicious location of the Kushana empire at the crossroads of Eurasia, at the center of the new trade routes that we know as the Silk Road, the influence of these intellectuals and Buddhist artisans would be felt throughout the Asian world.

LIFE AND ART OF THE SILK ROAD

The Silk Road offers an excellent illustration of the interrelationships and shared agency of Nayan Chanda's categories of global actors. During the first two centuries CE, the Silk Road emerged as a major route for traders linking the major centers of Eurasian civilization, facilitated by the expansive policies and diplomatic arrangements of warrior rulers and granting unprecedented new mobility to missionaries of several religious communities. This so-called Silk Road was not in fact a single route, nor did it remain stable throughout its existence, as the historian Xinru Liu observes (1998). (These trade routes received the romantic name Silk Road only in the late nineteenth century thanks to a German scholar, Ferdinand von Richthofen.) However, during the first millennium CE these routes would remain a significant pathway for material goods and cultural products between East and West until maritime trade routes began to supplant the overland caravan trade around the eleventh century.

The foundation of the Silk Road was desire: the desire of elites in one region to possess items of luxury and rarity from other regions, as a means of pleasure or a mark of status. Xinru Liu suggests that the trade may have begun with horses. The Chinese Han emperors sought to gain the especially fine "blood-sweat" horses bred in regions to the west of them and considered to be a divine species. They established garrisons along their western frontiers and made alliances with some of the smaller oasis-based kingdoms around the Taklamakan Desert in Central Asia. This early Chinese opening to the West soon brought more than horses to the elites of China. Furs and carpets arrived from Central Asia, cotton and precious gems from India, and glassware from the Mediterranean. Meanwhile, Roman elites developed a taste for the silk cloth that was then produced only in China. By the fourth or fifth century, India was producing its own silk, as were the Persians. Chinese silk had reached the Mediterranean via the coastal route through Southeast Asia and around the Indian peninsula, but in the first two centuries CE the volume of trade in this commodity increased dramatically. In Pliny's complaints about the negative balance of trade, he cited the Roman elite's desire for silk as one of the main culprits.

New technologies of transport no doubt facilitated the growth in the Asian caravan routes in the early centuries CE, as did a favorable political situation. Just as harnessing the monsoon allowed more efficient navigation across the Indian Ocean, advances in the harnessing and breeding of the camel helped make long-distance overland trade across Central Asia possible and profitable. Camels had been domesticated many centuries before, but the invention and spread of a new type of saddle, the North Arabian saddle, turned the camel into an ideal vehicle for the arid steppe lands. A single camel could carry from three hundred to five hundred pounds and forage for its food along the way. It became a veritable "ship of the desert" (Bulliet 1975: 164–65; McNeill 1987).

Stationed in the northwestern parts of the Indian subcontinent, the Kushana empire imposed itself in the middle of the emerging trade routes leading west out of China toward the Roman world. At the eastern end were the Chinese cities of Ch'ang-an and Loyang, while at the western terminus were cities such as Antioch and Tyre on the eastern coast of the Mediterranean, which served as entrepôts for the Roman trade. In between lay Central Asian oasis city-states such as Kucha and Turfan, whose economies and livelihoods came to depend on the trade caravans passing through. A major southward spur off the east-west routes led down through Bactria and Gandhara, overland to Mathura, and from there to Barygaza or Bharukaccha, then the largest port on the western coast of India. While maps of the Silk Road often depict just the east-west lines of trade, it is likely that during the first two centuries CE the majority of trade moved along this southern route through Kushana lands into India and then across the Indian Ocean to the Egyptian ports along the Red Sea (see map 3.2).[3]

The routes, in any case, were long and treacherous. In Central Asia and the northwestern parts of South Asia, the Silk Road traversed deserts and high mountain passes prone to unpredictable weather. Along the routes were oasis cities, which could pose their own problems. Local political changes in any stopping place along the route could result in new tariffs or detours. Caravans with their valuable cargoes were susceptible to Silk Road extortion. However, in the first two centuries CE the presence of stable large empires— the Roman, Parthian, Kushana, and Han Chinese—helped protect the traders from extortion by smaller rulers or bandits along the way. For the merchants and travelers it was a high-risk enterprise. Even with the excellent horses and stalwart camels of Central Asia to serve as pack animals, the volume of commodities transported was never large, and the trade therefore focused on the precious, the rare, and the easily portable. Gems and valuable ornamental objects such as coral, pearls, decorative glassware, perfumes, and incense made their way north and east to China while silk was the most notable Chinese export to India and the West. Some unique objects were destined for rulers, as gifts meant to establish or maintain political alliances. Other commodities made their way to wealthy elites in the cities of China, India, and the Mediterranean as conspicuous items of consumption and display. A goodly number ended up as devotional presentations to religious institutions, which especially in India became ostentatious during this period. Buddhist texts of this period direct devotees to decorate their stupas with silk bands and bells, canopies and banners, and to worship the Buddha in his image form with gems and jewels, necklaces, clothes, ointments, and much more. Not surprisingly, archaeological excavations of Buddhist stupas have often unearthed hoards of pearls, coral, glass beads, and other precious ornamental stones (Liu 1998: 11).

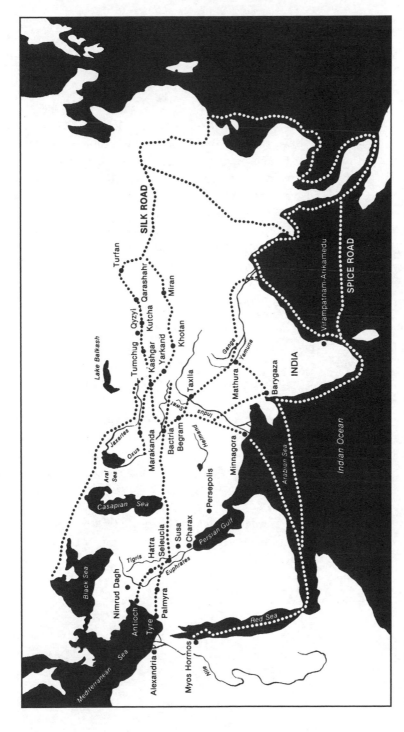

Map 3.2: Trade Routes between the Mediterranean and China during the Kushana Period. Reprinted from Stanislaw Czuma, *Kushan Sculpture* (1985). Map by Joseph Finizia. Reproduced courtesy of the Cleveland Museum of Art.

Along with the itinerant traders and their pack animals carrying precious commodities came itinerant Buddhist monks, carrying what they considered precious ideas. We have already seen how Buddhism was introduced into China by emigrants from India and the Central Asian city-states such as An Shih-kao from Parthia and Kumarajiva from Kucha. And later the same trade routes allowed Chinese Buddhist pilgrims such as Faxian to make their way to India. Oasis city-states on the Silk Road—Kucha, Turfan, Khotan, and others—developed their own thriving Buddhist communities. Monks found the nearby mountains, cliffs, and dramatic gorges suitable locations to carve out meditation cells and modest monastic centers. The solitude and the vast, silent landscape must have offered an inspiring site for meditation. Monks also translated key Buddhist works into local languages, and in some cases they composed new Buddhist works as well, which were then disseminated into India and China. Such fundamental Mahayana Buddhist works as the *Avatamsaka Sutra* and the *Lotus Sutra*, it has been argued, may have been written first in a Central Asian language and translated from that into both Sanskrit and Chinese (Poceski 2004: 341).

The trading cities along the Silk Road relied on the caravans that brought goods and people from many different cultures, and this must have encouraged a cosmopolitan atmosphere open to new groups and ideas. It is no accident, then, that texts by Zoroastrian, Manichean, and Nestorian Christian teachers have been found alongside Buddhist ones in Central Asian excavations. Nor did Buddhism remain unaffected by the ideas and practices of other religious communities. Although it is difficult to trace the lines of influence with certainty, many scholars of Buddhism have argued that several important new developments in Mahayana Buddhism, such as the cults of the new bodhisattvas Amitabha and Maitreya, show clear parallels with earlier Zoroastrian divinities. There is strong reason to believe that in the Silk Road settlements of Central Asia, as we have seen in China, Buddhism took on new forms through its encounters with other ideologies. Setting out from India, Buddhism had grown beyond its homeland.[4]

4

ADVENTURERS

In 1975 the Sahitya Akademi, an organization for the promotion of Indian literature supported by the Indian government, convened an International Ramayana Conference. Delegates came from Burma, India, Indonesia, Japan, Malaysia, Mongolia, the Philippines, Sri Lanka, and Thailand in Asia, as well as from Europe and the United States, to discuss a single shared story, the epic adventure of Prince Rama of Ayodhya. The most influential telling of Rama's story, the Sanskrit *Ramayana* attributed to Valmiki, was composed in northern India probably in the early centuries CE, though Valmiki's version drew on older oral legends. From its place of origin, the story spread. It was retold in every vernacular language of India, and it was adapted into languages and cultures far beyond the South Asian subcontinent. It has exercised a particularly powerful influence in Southeast Asia as far as the islands of Java and Bali in modern Indonesia. The list of delegates to the 1975 conference provides an index of the global distribution of this cultural product of classical India. Like a Bollywood blockbuster, albeit more slowly, the adventurous tale of Rama enchanted audiences as it journeyed throughout the Asian world.[1]

In this epic tale Prince Rama is an inadvertent adventurer. Exiled from his own kingdom, Rama travels far outside his home territory in north-central India. He encounters all sorts of strange creatures and cultures in his travels, including a society of talking monkeys and a sophisticated urban kingdom ruled by demons. If we read this epic allegorically, as I propose to do here, Valmiki's *Ramayana* is a narrative of global engagement that reflected the expansionary "civilizing mission" of a North Indian cultural and political order as it spread historically beyond its center in the Gangetic Plain. However, before we examine Rama's tale, let us reconsider the social map of South Asia during this period.

HOMELANDS AND THE FOREIGN

It is important to remember that the national boundaries of the modern world are not natural phenomena. They are the result of historical processes, often quite recent. The current borders of the South Asian nations owe their origins

45

to British colonial rule of the nineteenth and early twentieth centuries, to the partition of British India in 1947, and to the Bangladeshi war of independence in 1971. Nor are these borders completely stable and universally accepted, as can be seen in the continued dispute over Kashmir and the various secessionist movements of northeastern India. Our modern nations, it is clear, do not necessarily correspond to the geographical conceptions held by earlier inhabitants of South Asia.

In the early centuries CE, orthodox Brahman and Buddhist writers designated an area of central northern India, centered on the plain of the Ganges and Yamuna rivers, as Aryavarta (homeland of the Aryas) or Madhyadesha (the middle country). As the Dharmashastra of Manu, an orthodox Brahmanic work of this period, defines it, "From the eastern sea [the Bay of Bengal] to the western sea [the Arabian Sea], the area in between the two mountains [the Himalayas to the north and Vindhyas to the south] is what the wise men call the Land of the Aryans" (Doniger and Smith 1991: 19). They considered this large region to be a privileged zone of shared culture or civilization, which they identified with the adjective *arya*, often translated as "noble." In Brahmanical works such as Manu's treatise, the Aryavarta was a pure country where Brahmans could offer Vedic sacrifices and live according to the dharma, the code of proper or righteous conduct. "Where the black antelope ranges by nature," continues Manu, "that should be known as the country fit for sacrifices; and beyond it is the country of the barbarian (*mleccha*)."[2]

Manu uses a common term here, *mleccha* (usually translated, as here, as "barbarian"), to refer to all those who live outside the Aryavarta and do not share in the common social fabric of Arya culture. *Mleccha* does not point to a particular social group or community but rather can denote both "foreigners" from outside the subcontinent and "tribals" or other indigenous communities within South Asia not incorporated into the prevailing Arya cultural order. Thus Greek and Roman Yavanas from the Mediterranean world and Kushanas from Central Asia are sometimes referred to as *mlecchas*, along with the various hunter-gatherer, pastoral, and agricultural groups that inhabited the uncultivated hills and the plowed river valleys of central India. The term, as Aloka Parasher argues, is a pejorative one. Brahmanic, Buddhist, and Jain writers of this period all show a "vehement belief in the superiority of themselves vis-à-vis *mlecchas*."[3] The distinction they make between *arya* and *mleccha*, says Parasher, relies on three principal factors: language, place of habitation, and cultural behavior. It is not, he adds, a matter of religious, ethnic, or racial difference.

Considerations of *arya* and *mleccha* had particular relevance in the early centuries CE. As Parasher puts it, "[F]rom the beginning of the Christian era to the sixth century A.D., political events and external influence in all spheres of activity particularly during the initial stages, brought about a process of immediate change and disrupted old-established patterns of authority" (1991: 34). This period of change involved, as we have seen, intercontinental trading networks, pan-Asian religious missions, and the establishment of new kingdoms in India by warrior groups from outside the subcontinent. This was also a period of steady expansion in the reach of Arya culture. The black antelope, in Manu's metaphor for the lands of sacrificial purity, began to roam over larger portions of South Asia. As settlers from northern India began to spread into other parts of the subcontinent, they came into contact with peoples ranging from the hunter-gatherer tribes of the upland plateaus to the trading colonies along the coasts and the well-developed, agriculture-based chieftainships of Tamil Nadu. This expansion provoked lively debates over issues of cultural contact and hegemony. Could a *mleccha* become an *arya*? To what extent and under what conditions could others be incorporated into the Arya social order? How much leeway exists in the notion of dharma for the local customs of others? Do the principles of dharma apply to outsiders? Some argued for an exclusionary position. Manu and other Dharmashastra authors urged their orthodox audiences to adopt an attitude of passive avoidance toward outsiders. We will return to the localist ideology of Manu in the next chapter. Others, like Valmiki, had a more expansive and incorporative perspective.

We will examine Valmiki's telling of the adventurous travels of Prince Rama in light of these issues. Although this is an epic poem, not a factual travel account, Rama's tale offers much insight into the very real questions of cultural contact and social incorporation faced in the early centuries CE by those who called themselves Arya and those outside their social order.

RAMA'S JOURNEY BEYOND ARYAVARTA

Rama is the son of King Dasharatha, a king of the Kshatriya, or warrior class, ruling in Ayodhya, situated north of the Ganges on the Sarayu River in the heart of Aryavarta, present-day Uttar Pradesh. Even among royalty Rama is special. According to Valmiki, Rama and his three younger brothers are born out of a special child-producing Vedic sacrifice performed by Dasharatha. What is more, Valmiki informs us, Prince Rama is actually an incarnation (*avatara*) of the high god Vishnu, come to earth to restore dharma. Although Rama's divine identity is not generally recognized by other characters in the story, nor by Rama himself, it has a crucial bearing on the narrative.

As Rama grows up, he is trained in the arts of the warrior class and in the principles of proper conduct. He becomes an exemplary prince, as Valmiki elaborates:

> He was of noble descent on both sides of his family, he was upright and cheerful, truthful, and honest. Aged brahmans had seen to his training, men who were wise in the ways of righteousness and statecraft. And thus he understood the true nature of righteousness, statecraft, and personal pleasure. He was retentive and insightful, knowledgeable and adept in the social proprieties. . . . He could head a charge in battle and lead an army skillfully. He was invincible in combat, even if the gods and *asuras* [demons] themselves were to unite in anger against him. He was never spiteful, haughty, or envious, and he had mastered his anger. He would never look down on any creature nor bow to the will of time.[4]

As the oldest son of the chief queen and the most highly accomplished and virtuous of Dasharatha's sons, Rama appears destined to become the worthy successor to his father's throne. However, when Dasharatha decides to retire and appoint Rama as king, court jealousy and intrigue intervene to alter his plan. At the determined insistence of Kaikeyi, one of Dasharatha's younger wives, the king is forced to send Rama into exile for fourteen years and to make one of Rama's younger brothers, Kaikeyi's son Bharata, ruler in his stead. Rama obediently acquiesces to this shift. Dasharatha's expulsion of Rama leads the hero on an epic adventure far beyond the familiar world of Ayodhya and Arya culture.

When Rama, accompanied by his wife Sita and his devoted brother Lakshmana, crosses the Ganges River and heads south, he enters a new and exotic world. The translator Sheldon Pollock likens it to Alice's falling down the rabbit hole into Wonderland. Valmiki's narrative takes the intrepid trio southward across the Vindhya mountains to the Deccan Plateau, where they spend over ten years in the Dandaka Forest along the upper reaches of the Godavari River in present-day Maharashtra. Farther south, Rama and Lakshmana spend more time in Kishkindha along the upper Krishna River in modern Karnataka. Finally, to recover Sita, who has been abducted, they mount a military campaign all the way to Sri Lanka off the southeastern tip of India (see map 4.1). As they venture farther from the Aryavarta, well beyond where the black antelope roams, they encounter not only the wolves, tigers, and other wild animals one might expect in the forest but also stranger creatures such as talking vultures, sociable monkeys, and shape-shifting demons. Valmiki portrays the territories south of Aryavarta as a realm of the fantastic. Yet Rama's encounters there also allow Valmiki and his readers to reflect on issues of Otherness.

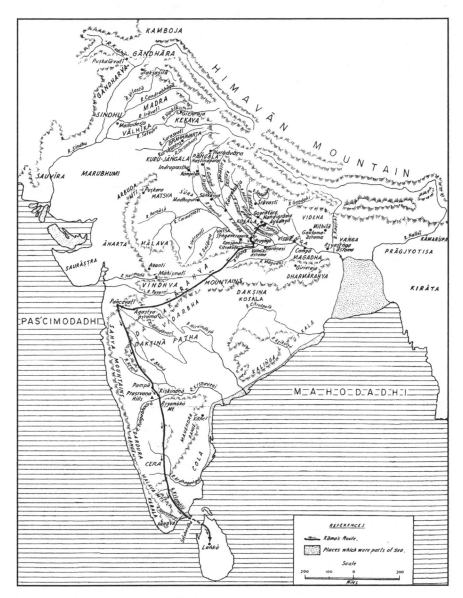

Map 4.1: India in the Ramayana Age. Reprinted from S. N. Vyas, *India in the Ramayana Age*, 1967.

Encounters Outside Aryavarta

Three categories of other beings that Rama encounters outside his homeland are of particular importance to the *Ramayana*: the Brahman ascetics of the Dandaka Forest; the demons, or Rakshasas, who have their capital in Lanka; and the monkeys of Kishkindha.

In the Dandaka Forest, human sages (*munis*) live in small clustered communities called ashrams.[5] They wear clothes of bark and dwell in simple huts made of leaves. Members of the Brahman class, they occupy themselves with the practices of reciting the Vedas and offering Vedic sacrifices, the most sacred activities of the Brahman class within traditional Arya culture. They all live in an austere manner, and many also perform acts of still greater austerity. Some subsist entirely on leaves, Valmiki reports, or only on water, or even on air alone. Some sleep only on the ground. Others stand upright surrounded by four fires, with the sun overhead as the fifth in the "five-five vow." Through their virtuous lives and rigorous practices they come to glow with "brahmanical majesty" and seek to generate "ascetic power." Tales are told of the great potency of this power. It may force even the gods to comply with the commands of the ascetics.

Living far from the settled kingdoms of northern India, the inhabitants of the Dandaka ashrams are vulnerable. As Rama visits the hermitages, the sages repeatedly complain of attacks by Rakshasas, a class of "night-stalking" demons who disrupt their sacrificial rites and slaughter the sacrificers. They address Rama as a member of the warrior class, reminding him that a Kshatriya ruler is responsible for the protection and security of all those within his domain, and they appeal to him for help. Even though Rama is not technically king and the sages do not live within the Ayodhya kingdom or even in Aryavarta, Rama agrees—against the anxious warnings of his wife— to extend his protection to the defenseless sages. For over ten years Rama and his companions travel from ashram to ashram in the Dandaka Forest as guardians for the Brahman sages. This brings him into inexorable conflict with the Rakshasas.

Valmiki's fictional narrative reflects a real historical pattern of this period. In the early centuries CE small groups of Brahmans often did venture out beyond the areas of sedentary agriculture and settled kingdoms and acted as "pioneers into wild territory," as the historian D. D. Kosambi puts it.[6] They migrated as peaceful settlers in small unarmed groups to establish ashrams for Vedic instruction and recitation. These uncultivated borderlands or forests were often inhabited by nomadic hunter-gatherer or pastoral groups that were not part of the Arya social order. Kosambi suggests that the Brahman settlers, like cultural missionaries, often interacted with these indigenous groups, both by introducing new practices such as plow agriculture and by incorporating local rites or deities into an assimilative Hindu culture. Nothing guaranteed that the interlopers would receive a warm welcome when they moved into territories already occupied by others, however. If threatened by indigenous groups, these Brahman missionaries might call on the protection of distant warriors or kings, which could lead to political incorporation of the territory into an existing kingdom. This is what is happening with the sages of the Dandaka Forest and the exiled prince Rama. In the fictional world of the *Ramayana*, however, the creatures threatening the Brahman pioneers are more powerful than mere human tribesmen.

The Rakshasas, or "night stalkers," are a class of demons or nongods (*asuras*), beings with superhuman powers who are opposed to the Vedic or Hindu gods (*devas*). They are described as *kamarupin*, that is, they can take on whatever form they wish, and in the course of the story they often do. In the *Ramayana*, the Rakshasas first appear as aggressive opponents of the Brahman ascetics who have established ashrams in the hinterlands. They especially despise the Vedic sacrifices. The Rakshasas dump blood and raw meat onto the sacrificial fires and violently attack the sacrificers. An army of fourteen thousand Rakshasas has been deputed to the Dandaka Forest specifically to harass the newcomers. Another important characteristic of the Rakshasas is their uninhibited sexuality. After Rama has defended the sages' ashrams, he is accosted by a female Rakshasi, Shurpanakha. When Rama rejects her sexual overtures, Shurpanakha immediately shifts her attention to his brother Lakshmana. Less self-controlled than Rama, Lakshmana responds to the advances of the demoness by cutting off her ears and nose.

The first demons Rama encounters in the forest appear alone as isolated rangers, but the Rakshasas also have an organized society and political system with its capital in Lanka. Valmiki portrays Lanka as a glittering city full of towering, luxurious mansions, every bit as magnificent as Ayodhya. There live the Rakshasa elite, "a class of beautiful and cultivated, if highly sensual, beings who live lives of luxury and indulgence," as translators Robert and Sally Goldman put it (1996: 66). Valmiki's depiction of Lanka complicates any superficial assumption that demons are unequivocally evil; in many ways Rakshasa society parallels that of the human Ayodhya. As in the Arya society of Ayodhya, the Rakshasa society of Lanka is organized hierarchically, and its political system is a monarchy. The Rakshasa ruler Ravana maintains a harem of wives, like Dasharatha in Ayodhya (but unlike the determinedly monogamous Rama), and he also has a council of ministers with whom he consults on matters of state. Among the council members is Ravana's brother-in-law Vibhishana, a Rakshasa who recognizes the principles of righteous conduct (*dharma*) and consistently tries to direct his brother toward proper moral policies. However, Ravana just as consistently ignores or overrules Vibhishana's sound advice. Ravana's statecraft is governed not by dharma but rather by his sexual desires, arrogance, and use of brute force to achieve his ends. When Shurpanakha returns to Lanka, humiliated and mutilated, and complains to her brother, Ravana's vengefulness and sexual acquisitiveness lead him to seize Rama's beautiful wife Sita by force and hold her captive in Lanka.

When Sita is abducted, the fortunes of Rama reach a low ebb. Deprived of kingship, exiled from home, and now bereft of his wife, Rama nearly goes mad. He and Lakshmana are reduced to wandering about the forest looking for signs that might tell them in which direction Sita has been taken. A friendly vulture provides the first clue, and a helpful Rakshasa assists them further. Traveling farther south into the area around Lake Pampa, they come across the monkeys of Kishkindha. For Rama, meeting the monkeys marks a turning point in his fortunes.

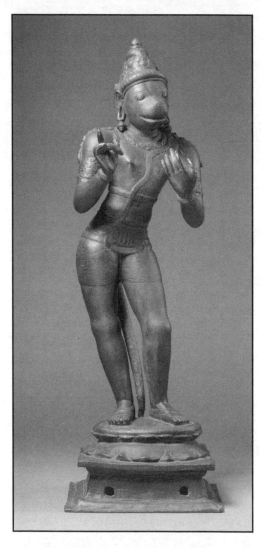

Figure 4.1: Standing Hanuman (Chola period, Tamilnad, eleventh century). *Source:* Metropolitan Museum of Art. Image © Metropolitan Museum of Art, New York.

The monkeys (*vanara*) are forest-dwelling creatures with fur and tails. They can leap great distances and climb trees with great skill, just like the monkeys one finds throughout southern India today. However, in many other respects the monkeys of the *Ramayana* resemble humans. They have speech. One of them, Hanuman, is particularly known for his eloquent Sanskrit and diplomatic skills (see figure 4.1). The monkeys wear clothing and ornaments. In another respect they are similar to the Rakshasas: they, too, are said to be *kamarupin*, capable of shifting shape.

The monkeys are organized politically as a monarchy, much like the humans of Ayodhya and the Rakshasas of Lanka. The ruler of this monkey kingdom sits on a throne, with all the regalia of a human sovereign, in a splendid palace at the center of a magnificent capital city, although this capital, Kishkindha, is inside a mountain cave. Like Dasharatha and Ravana, the king here maintains many wives in his women's quarters. He has a council of ministers and monkey-Brahman priests who perform the royal consecration and other public ceremonies. The monkey society of Kishkindha, as Valmiki portrays it, provides a mirror image of a human society, but it is a distorted reflection, as Rama soon discovers.

Unlike the Rakshasas, the monkeys do not harbor any particular hostility toward Brahmans or other humans. Rama is able to form an alliance with the Kishkindha monkey kingdom, and with its substantial assistance he locates Sita and ultimately defeats Ravana and the Rakshasa forces. In the end he recovers his wife. However, to gain the help of these monkey forces Rama must first interfere in their political affairs, and his intervention is not without its problems.

Who were the Rakshasas? And who were the monkeys of Kishkindha, really? Many scholars of India have attempted to identify the Rakshasas and monkeys of the *Ramayana* as particular historical ethnic or religious groups. Thus the Rakshasas have been identified as various Dravidian and tribal groups of southern India, as the Buddhists of Sri Lanka, or even as Australian aborigines. The monkeys are said to be specific tribal peoples of the Deccan highlands, some of whom, it has been postulated, may have had monkeylike tails.[7] The recent translators of Valmiki's epic have rightly criticized these overly literal efforts to turn the great poem into a narrative of real historical events. As Robert Goldman puts it, "We are convinced that attempts at an ethnological identification of the *raksasas* and the *vanaras* and the geographical location of their strongholds are not only futile but wrongheaded. For in seeking a historical basis for what is, in many respects, a kind of elaborate fairy tale, we are led away from a true understanding of the work" (1984: 28). However, a preemptive assignment of the epic to the fairy tale realm of the imagination also, I believe, precludes a true understanding of a major aspect of the work, namely, the poet's serious reflections on political encounters with Others. The Rakshasas and monkeys of the *Ramayana* are not just objects of fantasy but also creatures in whose societies the protagonist intervenes. In both cases Rama evaluates individual leaders, forms alliances, uses violence to depose kings, and installs new rulers who owe loyalty to him as a patron. While it is not a direct transcription of reality, the epic does provide a fictional narrative for thinking about real historical encounters as Arya culture spread beyond Aryavarta. Valmiki was particularly concerned with the role of dharma when dealing with social groups outside the Arya fold.

INTERVENTIONS AND MORALITY

Like all adventurers who journey beyond their homelands, Rama enters the Dandaka Forest, Kishkindha, and Lanka as new territories already inhabited by other creatures. He interacts with those already there, and his actions change things. In the *Ramayana,* Valmiki narrates Rama's interventions, and he also allows the characters to reflect on and discuss the morality of these actions.

In fact, social transformations are occurring before Rama arrives in the Dandaka Forest. Brahman ascetic groups have moved into the territory to establish ashrams for their Vedic practices. Rakshasa patrols, some under Ravana's command, are aggressively attacking these newcomers. Although the Rakshasas do not appear to claim the forest as part of their settled dominion, they clearly resent the intrusion of the settlers from northern India. When Rama and Lakshmana visit the forest hermitages, the Brahmans request Rama's protection from their assailants. By complying, Rama is assisting in the initial spread of Arya cultural forms in a new region. This leads to further encounters with members of the Rakshasa royal family. After Lakshmana disfigures Surpanakha and Rama decimates a troop of fourteen thousand Rakshasa rangers, Ravana escalates the hostilities by abducting Rama's wife and imprisoning her in Lanka. This sets the stage for the central conflict of the epic, the confrontation between the exiled Ayodhya prince Rama, exemplar of the Arya code of dharma, and the demonic emperor of Lanka, Ravana, who is in many ways the antithesis of a dharmic ruler. However, before this struggle can play itself out, Rama must intervene in another community, the monkey kingdom of Kishkindha.

When Rama arrives in the Kishkindha region, searching for the trail of Sita, he does not immediately approach the ruler of the monkeys, Valin. Rather, he meets with Sugriva, the king's aggrieved younger brother, who is hiding from Valin in a cave with a few retainers. Sugriva explains his situation to Rama. He had replaced his brother on the throne temporarily while Valin was fighting a demon in a cave and had erroneously assumed that Valin was dead. When the older brother returned after defeating the demon, Valin had treated Sugriva as a usurper. He forced Sugriva into exile and kept Sugriva's wife. As one wifeless exile to another, Rama and Sugriva quickly strike up a friendship and reverently circumambulate a fire to solemnize their alliance.

The two allies are not exactly alike, however. Rama gracefully acquiesced in his younger brother's assumption of the Ayodhya throne while Sugriva is resentful toward his older brother and ambitious to regain kingship over Kishkindha. He requests that Rama assist him in a plan to defeat Valin, and, observing the code of friendship, Rama agrees even before he knows the full story. Sugriva proposes to invite Valin to a fight. Knowing that Valin will accept this challenge, Sugriva asks Rama to hide nearby and shoot Valin while the two monkeys struggle. Monkeys fight hand-to-hand or by swinging clubs; Rama possesses the more potent long-distance military technology of the bow and arrow. The monkeys wrestle ferociously, and just as Valin is about to subdue Sugriva, Rama shoots his deadly arrow.

Valin does not expire directly. In the past he has received a special life-extending necklace from the god Indra, and this gift allows him the opportunity to reproach Rama for intervening in monkey affairs. The dialogue between the dying Valin and victorious Rama occupies two substantial chapters in Valmiki's narrative, and it raises key questions about the universality of dharma and the relations between humans and monkey societies.

Valin begins by contrasting Rama's reputation for virtue with his ignoble conduct. Warriors both human and monkey accept that it is unfair to shoot someone from hiding. Further, Valin questions the reasons for Rama's involvement in the monkey kingdom. He has not harmed Rama or his kingdom, and, since monkeys are forest-dwelling creatures who subsist on roots and nuts, they do not threaten human settlements. The monkeys, Valin suggests, are not the aggressors here, and so there is no call for retribution. And since Rama does not eat monkey meat or wear monkey fur, he cannot justify his slaughter of Valin in the terms humans normally use to rationalize hunting other forest animals. From Valin's point of view, Rama's intervention and his tactics both contradict his stature as an exemplar of dharma.

Rama responds by chastising Valin. The monkey, he asserts, does not understand dharma or other Arya values. First of all, the earth itself belongs to his dynasty, he claims, and he was simply acting on behalf of the current ruler in Ayodhya, his brother Bharata. After this overarching claim to imperial dominion, Rama observes that Valin has not followed the "path of kings." By living with Sugriva's wife, says Rama, Valin has departed from dharma, and this transgression warrants Rama's punishment. Furthermore, Rama defends his conduct by invoking his alliance. He had promised Sugriva his help, and he always keeps his word. Dharma requires that one assist one's friends and that one's words remain truthful. Finally, Rama points out that humans trap and shoot animals by stealth, and after all Valin is only a monkey. At this point Valin admits that he is a lowly creature, and he accepts Rama's assertions about dharma. Rama consoles the dying monkey and tells him that he has now returned to dharma.

If the *Ramayana* is treated as an allegorical text, how should we view this deathbed dialogue? Through the voice of Valin, Valmiki raises cautionary issues that question the propriety of Rama's conduct, but the force of the narrative supports Rama's position. By claiming sovereignty far beyond the ordinary boundaries of Ayodhya or Aryavarta, Rama argues that it is legitimate for Arya warriors to intervene in other communities. The principles of dharma are universal, he suggests. They apply even to monkeys. This implies that other communities can become part of the Arya cultural order. However, monkeys such as Valin are inferior beings whose understanding of dharma is imperfect, and so it is proper that they occupy a subordinate role in the social hierarchy. As Kosambi and many other historians have observed, this was a common pattern of cultural assimilation by means of which outside groups became part of the Indian system of classes and monarchical states. "The chief, with the backing of a few nobles freed from tribal law," writes Kosambi (1965: 171), "would become ruler over his former tribe while the ordinary tribesman merged into the new peasantry."

Politically speaking, Rama gains a valuable ally through his actions. When Valin expires, Rama immediately has his friend Sugriva crowned as the new king of Kishkindha. Monkeys are capricious and pleasure-loving creatures, and at first Sugriva seems to be an imperfect supporter. While Rama wants the monkeys to conduct searches for his missing wife, Sugriva enjoys the pleasures of court life, and finally Rama must send Lakshmana to threaten the monkey ruler into action. Once roused, the monkeys prove to be formidable helpers. The alliance with the monkeys proves to be crucial to Rama's larger campaign against the Rakshasas.

There is no ambiguity in the case of the Rakshasas. In Valmiki's telling, Ravana's abduction of Sita clearly warrants Rama's retributive attack on Lanka. But here, too, Rama finds an ally among the Rakshasa royal family. As Rama and his monkey troops make camp on the shore near Lanka island, Ravana holds court among his advisers in the Rakshasa capital. Ravana's brother Vibhishana, who often speaks up for the values of dharma within the Rakshasa court, repeatedly urges the ruler to return Sita and avoid a war that is sure to be cataclysmic. Harshly rebuked by Ravana, Vibhishana flees Lanka and seeks refuge in Rama's camp. His arrival prompts a lengthy debate among the monkey leadership about his intentions, but, as the diplomat Hanuman correctly discerns, Vibhishana has heard about Rama's support for another disinherited younger brother and has come seeking both asylum and a kingdom. Rama receives Vibhishana in friendship. Even before the attack on Lanka, Rama has Vibhishana ceremonially consecrated as king of the Rakshasas, a symbolic indication of his aim. In the course of battle, Vibhishana's knowledge of Rakshasa weapons and tactics proves invaluable to Rama's cause. And when the Rakshasa army is decimated and Ravana finally slain on the battlefield, Rama commands that his ally Vibhishana be crowned king of Lanka as soon as possible. Again, Rama has deposed a sitting ruler and installed a younger member of the royal family who owes loyalty to him.

In the contrasting examples of the monkeys and the Rakshasa, Rama's actions illustrate two types of intervention. With the monkeys he is able to effect a relatively peaceful coup d'état and enlist the monkeys as warriors in his own campaign. With the Rakshasas, by contrast, nothing less than a fierce war can succeed in bringing this kingdom into submission. However, in both cases the result is assimilation and alliance with Ayodhya.

After his victory over Ravana and his recovery of Sita, Rama returns to Ayodhya and finally, after his fourteen-year absence, assumes the throne. During the ceremonies of installation, Valmiki relates, Rama's closest attendants are his three brothers and two new allies, the rulers of Kishkindha and Lanka. Sugriva and Vibhishana hold the yak-tail fly whisks that betoken their fealty to their overlord Rama. The formerly independent kingdoms of the monkeys and Rakshasas are now subordinate parts of the Ayodhya empire ruled by Rama. Valmiki's telling of Rama's journey into southern India as far as Lanka begins as a tale of fantastic adventure but ends also as a narrative of political integration.

5

LOCALISTS

In the early centuries CE, expanding long-distance trade routes, both sea-based and overland, connected India with other parts of the known world from Rome to China. Missionaries took the teaching of the Buddha Shakyamuni from the Gangetic valley, where he had lived, to every part of Asia and in their journeys interacted with those professing myriad other faiths. Warrior groups like the Kushanas came into the subcontinent to establish new empires that integrated territories far north and west of India with those in the Gangetic region. Stories of travel and epics of adventure narrated the dangers and rewards in the expanding horizons of the known. These globalizing movements introduced not just new trade commodities but also new peoples, ideas, and social arrangements into Indian society.

As Nayan Chanda points out, globalization does not favor everyone, and this holds true for South Asia during this period. We have seen already how the narratives of the time acknowledged the dangers involved in journeying beyond one's safe homeland. The story literature often allegorizes the dangers of travel in the form of other categories of beings, sometimes benign but often threatening. Out there are female Yakshis who seduce and then devour helpless sailors, Nagas who defend their lands from Buddhist preachers, and fearsome Rakshasas who attack the sacrifices of Brahman pioneers. We have also seen the cultural distinctions that those who considered themselves *arya* made between themselves and those *mlecchas* they held to be outside the pale of Aryavarta. But the dangers, for some localists, could also lie close to home in the kinds of social changes that threatened the status quo.

The Dharmashastra literature of the period provides a fuller articulation of this localist perspective. The Dharmashastras of Manu, Yajnavalkya, and others are treatises that set forth the social and moral vision of orthodox Brahmans who remained, during a period of profound change, loyal to older Vedic principles and ways of life.[1] They envisioned an organic social order composed of four primary classes (*varnas*) that originated from a single unitary being, and they prescribed detailed codes for proper or righteous conduct (*dharma*), based, they claimed, on the ancient sacred Vedas and the model behavior of exemplary Brahmans. The aim of these works was to outline a complex conception of dharma as it applies differently to different classes of society and to those at different stages of life (*asrama*). The Dharmashastras present a compelling vision of a harmonious social order based on eternal values. However, it was an exclusive order.

In Manu's Dharmashastra, as in many other texts of this period, the Aryavarta is viewed as a privileged zone of sacrificial purity, set off from the outside world inhabited by others. Manu advises those who maintain the highest standards, namely, Brahmans and other pious twice-born beings, to remain in this region: "The twice-born should make every effort to settle in these countries; but a servant [member of the lowest class] may live in any country at all if he is starved for a livelihood" (Doniger and Smith 1991: 19). This geographical preference for the land of the Aryas was not limited to the orthodox. Buddhist and Jain texts sometimes give similar advice. The underlying idea is that contact with outsiders may lead to impurity. It is not a matter of active aggression toward *mlecchas*. But to maintain personal purity and righteous conduct, Manu advises, Brahmans should adopt a policy of passive avoidance. They should avoid living in *mleccha* lands, they should avoid speaking *mleccha* languages, and they should exclude *mlecchas* from their Vedic ceremonies. Similarly, the Brahman should avoid the one who travels to foreign lands by sea. The Dharmashastra authors adopt a similar posture of exclusion toward those they label *nastikas* (atheists), a category that includes the heterodox Buddhists and Jains.

We can contrast this insular view of dharma with the more outward-oriented perspective of Valmiki's *Ramayana*. The author of the epic argues for a conception of dharma that is universal. For Valmiki, principles of dharma apply even to monkeys and Rakshasas, although these creatures may fail to understand properly or act accordingly. This conviction of a far-reaching dharma gives Rama a guide for his interactions with others beyond Aryavarta. Ultimately this leads to the incorporation of those Others into Rama's own dominion. Although Manu also recognizes some universal principles of dharma, he is more concerned to delineate a situation-specific set of guidelines, especially as they apply to Brahman males. For Manu and other Dharmashastra authors, this is the way to conserve the worthy Vedic tradition, a system of permanent cultural values and clear social roles. The alternative, as they see it, is a precipitous decline in social cohesion leading to a state of anarchy (*kaliyuga*). For many who felt threatened by the social changes of the period, the Dharmashastra of Manu must have been a reassuring and persuasive vision of stability.

With Manu and the Dharmashastra vision, we come full circle to Henry Kissinger's stereotype of India as "a world apart," insular and unchanging. The Dharmashastra of Manu was among the very first Sanskrit texts to be translated into English. William Jones, chief justice of the Supreme Court in Calcutta, translated it in 1794, at a time when the newly established British colonial rulers of eastern India sought to locate the permanent law codes of India and administer justice according to those laws. The use of classical Dharmashastras for colonial period jurisprudence was not successful, and the British soon abandoned it. However, Manu's text has been regularly cited since, not as a conservative voice of protest from the early centuries CE but as a reliable description of Indian realities. Later historians have often viewed the Dharmashastra presentation of a self-sufficient, small-scale, stable, and virtuous social world as a reflection of a persistent Indian social reality. From the misreading of ancient and classical Indian texts such as the Manu Dharmashastra have come the historical misrepresentations and stereotypes that Henry Kissinger and many others have repeated.

The historical picture of India during the early centuries CE that we have viewed in this booklet appears significantly different. Following Nayan Chanda's scheme of four main types of globalizing agents, we have looked at the way traders linked the Indian subcontinent into a "world system" of commerce reaching from Rome to China, with India a central node on both the sea and land routes. We have observed the development of Buddhism as a pan-Asian missionary faith with a universalizing message that took on new forms as it was integrated itself in new cultural settings and interacted with other religious beliefs and practices. Among warriors we have focused on the Kushanas, who began as nomads migrating from western China and established a large new empire that united northern India with portions of Central Asia. In the process, we have seen, they helped promote the trade routes we know as the Silk Road and assisted in the Asian expansion of the Buddhist religion. Finally, we saw in the story of the exemplary adventurer Rama, hero of the epic *Ramayana*, an allegory of the gradual expansion of Arya cultural forms from northern India throughout the subcontinent and of the sometimes conflictual incorporation of other groups into the Hindu social order.

This is only one period in Indian history, of course, but the processes of interaction and exchange between India and other parts of the world have continued, while taking new forms and directions. A survey of the centuries following the first two CE, for example, would show even more intense interactions among Chinese, Central Asian, and Indian Buddhists and the growth of the university-like monasteries in India that became magnets for students throughout Asia. During this period, too, one would observe continuing trade routes around the Indian Ocean (though without Roman participation) and increasing connections between India and newly forming states in Southeast Asia, to which both Buddhist and Hindu specialists exported their cultural and religious ideas and practices. By the eighth century CE, the rise of another missionary religion, Islam, and the rapid expansion of new kingdoms that adhered to Islamic ideas laid the foundation of a new world system. Through Arab trading communities, energetic Sufi orders and shrines, and the roles of warriors affiliated with Islam in founding new states, India once again became a key part of a broader transcontinental network reaching from the Iberian Peninsula and northern Africa across the Middle East and South Asia as far as Indonesia. In his book title *When Asia Was the World,* Stewart Gordon aptly conveys the character of the thousand-year period between 500 and 1500.[2]

From 1493, when the Portuguese adventurer Vasco da Gama first landed along the same southeastern coast of India where the Greco-Roman Yavanas had traded in the early centuries CE, a new period in Indian history began. While for several hundred years South Asia remained closely connected to political and religious developments in the Islamic world, European merchants, missionaries, adventurers, warriors, and administrators would play a role in gradually incorporating India once again into a new European colonial world system. At no time in the history of South Asia would Kissinger's phrase "a world apart" truly apply.

GLOSSARY

Arya: Sanskrit term for "noble"

Aryavarta: geographical designation for the "homeland" of the Aryas, corresponding to central northern India in early centuries CE

Ashoka: Mauryan emperor of the third century BCE and paradigm of a Buddhist monarch

Bodhisattva: a person bound for enlightenment, one who assists others in attaining enlightenment

Brahman: the priestly and intellectual class in the early Indian scheme of classes

Dharma: code of proper conduct; righteousness or religious virtue

Dharmashastra: a genre of treatises outlining proper and righteous conduct for the various classes in early India

Duttagamini: ruler in Sri Lanka in the second century BCE who united the island under a single rule and patronized Buddhist institutions

Faxian: Chinese Buddhist monk who traveled to India and wrote an account of his journey

Funan: earliest known political kingdom in Southeast Asia located in coastal Vietnam and Cambodia

Kshatriya: warrior and royal class in the early Indian scheme of classes

Kumarajiva: translator of Buddhist texts into Chinese

Kushana empire: Major South Asian kingdom in the first and second centuries CE with capitals in Purushapura and Mathura

Land of Gold (*suvarnabhumi*): legendary destination for South Asian traders, across the ocean, identified with various locations in Southeast Asia

Mahayana: the "Great Vehicle" of Buddhism

Manu: attributed author of a celebrated Dharmashastra, or treatise on proper conduct

Mauryan empire: major empire in South Asia founded in the fourth century BCE by Chandragupta with its capital at Pataliputra

Menander: Indo-Greek ruler and Buddhist patron based in Bactria in the second century BCE

Mleccha: term for those outside the Aryan cultural order, often translated as "barbarian"

Naga: snake; mythical snakelike semidivine figures in early Indian literature and lore

Rakshasa (male) and Rakshasi (female): "night-stalking" demons, principal antagonists in the *Ramayana*

Ramayana: Sanskrit epic poem, ascribed to Valmiki, which tells the adventures of Rama

Sangha: the Buddhist Order of monks and nuns or more generally the entire Buddhist community

Silk Road: series of trade routes through Central Asia linking China, South Asia, and the Mediterranean from about the first century CE

Valmiki: attributed author of the *Ramayana*

Vidyadhara (male) and Vidyadhari (female): mythical semidivine figures in early Indian literature

Yaksha (male) and Yakshi (female): semidivine nature spirits in early Indian literature

Yavana: term for Greek and Roman traders in South Asia, also applied to other "outsiders" from the West

Yuezhi: tribal group from China that migrated through Central Asia; founders of the Kushana empire

NOTES

INTRODUCTION

[1] Kissinger 1979: 842. I am grateful to Thomas Trautmann for bringing this work to my attention.

[2] Ibid., 843. For a more recent example of the enduring notion among the American foreign policy elite of "Hindu India" as a persistent, unchanging civilizational unity, see the widely discussed work of Samuel P. Huntington, *The Clash of Civilizations and the Remaking of World Order* (1996), 45.

[3] The best general social and political history for this period is Thapar 2002: 209–79. A briefer overview may be found in Kulke and Rothermund 1986: 49–108.

CHAPTER 1

[1] Roman trade with India has received a good deal of scholarly attention. E. H. Warmington's *The Commerce between the Roman Empire and India* ([1928] 1974) is an early and still valuable overview. More recent survey works include Sidebotham 1986; Young 2001; and Ray 2003: 165–87; as well as the collection of essays in Begley and DePuma 1991. In his introduction to the translation of the *Periplus Maris Erythraei*, Lionel Casson (1989) also provides a brief authoritative account of the trade.

[2] The Tamil term *yavanar* and Sanskrit *yavana* derive from *Ionian* and were probably adapted into Indic languages from the Persian. In the early centuries CE its usage was generally restricted to Greeks and Romans from the Mediterranean world, but in later times *Yavana* became a more general term for foreigners of various sorts (Selby 2008: 82).

[3] Jones 1917: 377–79. Other classical writers credit Hippalos as having been the first westerner to discover the navigational use of the monsoon, but, as Casson (1989) notes, Indian and Arab sailors were already making use of it.

[4] The Indian cotton industry would continue as a mainstay of the international trade. Chanda writes that, "until the Industrial Revolution, Indian-made textiles remained the biggest major manufacturing export in the world. Cotton textile was the main engine behind India's accounting for nearly 25 percent of the world's gross domestic product in 1700" [(2007: 75)], not bad for a lethargic world apart.

[5] See Wheeler 1954 and Begley 1996 for valuable overviews of the excavations at Arikamedu. Begley notes that Arikamedu is the most important excavated

archaeological site in India for the study of overseas trade in the "Indo-Roman" period.

[6] Nathan Katz (2000: 9–30) argues persuasively for the plausibility of local traditions among the Jews of Kochi that trace their origins back to the dispersal of Jews from Palestine following the Roman destruction of the Second Temple in Jerusalem in 70 CE.

[7] A valuable and accessible item-by-item history of the international trade in spices is found in Dalby 2000. These Molucca Islands spices also entered the Indian marketplace. Andrew Dalby quotes the classical Indian medical text *Carakasamhita* on the benefits of spices: "One who wants clean, fresh, fragrant breath must keep nutmeg and cloves in the mouth" (2000:50).

[8] Versions of the legend show up in the Chinese chronicles, as well as later Champa inscriptions. Jan Przyluski has observed that this is a common foundation motif throughout the early Southeast Asian states and also appears in the foundational narratives of some Indian dynasties (1925 2:275–78).

[9] Historians of early Southeast Asia have long debated the degree of Indian impact on the new states of the region. Indian nationalist historians such as R. C. Majumdar (1985) wrote of "Indian colonies," and viewed states such as Funan as part of "Greater India." The French historian Georges Coedes ([1944] 1968) characterized the process as one of the "Indianization" of Southeast Asia. More recently O. W. Wolters (1982) and others have stressed the indigenous influence over the Indic in forming early Southeast Asian culture. In important recent studies, Sheldon Pollock (1996, 2006) has discussed the expansive role of the Sanskrit language during the first millennium CE in integrating South Asia and much of Southeast Asia into a single civilizational zone at an elite level, which he calls the "Sanskrit cosmopolis." Hall's "marriage of interests" points to a middle ground in this debate.

[10] Paul Wheatley (1961, 1983) provides the best starting point for an investigation of the Indic literature of the Land of Gold. He lists numerous sources and reviews other scholarly attempts to locate it. The tradition has repercussions up to the present day. It is no accident that Thailand named the airport in Bangkok, the prime point of entry for modern international tourists, the Suvarnabhoomi Airport.

[11] This resume of themes from the classical Indian tales of the Land of Gold draws from the Pali Buddhist stories known as *jatakas* (Cowell 1957), the Sanskrit Buddhist *Jatakamala* of Aryasura (Speyer 1895; Khoroche 1989), the Sanskrit Jain story collection *Kathakosa* (Tawney 1895), the Sanskrit secular story collections *Brhatkathaslokasamgraha* (Van Buitenen 1959) and the *Kathasaritsagara* of Somadeva (Tawney 1924–28), and the Tamil Jain epic *Civakacintamani* of Tiruttakkatevar (Ryan 2005).

CHAPTER 2

[1] The Thomas tradition is plausible but not universally accepted. All historians, however, agree that Christianity was present in southern India by the fourth century. See Panicker 2001.

[2] *Mahavamsa,* chaps. 22–32, translated in Geiger 1912: 146–227. Also see Smith 1978 on the subsequent influential role of the Duttagamini story in Southeast Asian history.

[3] Horner 1963. Most scholars presume that the text we have today is a later composition, or recension, perhaps from the first century CE. On Menander's career, see Narain 1957: 74–100.

[4] Zürcher 1972 is the standard scholarly work on this subject. Ch'en 1964 provides a more accessible treatment.

CHAPTER 3

[1] See "Possible Migration Routes of Central Asian Peoples to N.W. South Asia," plate III.C.1 (A) in Schwartzberg [1978] 1992: 20.

[2] Among the most important arguments in this debate, Alfred Foucher (1917) argued vigorously for a Gandharan (and ultimately Greek) origin of the Buddha image while A. K. Coomaraswamy (1927) just as vigorously supported Mathura. In the early twentieth century, the controversy often reflected colonial and nationalistic subtexts, with European scholars favoring the more "Western" style of Gandhara and Indians arguing for the indigenous Mathura style.

[3] Liu 1988: 19. For general comments on the mapping of the early Silk Road and its shifting pathways, see Liu 1988: 25–52.

[4] Clough n.d. I am grateful to Bradley Clough for consulting with me on Buddhist matters and for sharing his unpublished manuscript with me.

CHAPTER 4

[1] See Raghavan 1980 for the papers from this conference. On the broader terrain of the Rama story, see Raghavan 1980; and Richman 1991.

[2] Doniger and Smith 1991: 19. The Sanskrit term *arya,* unfortunately, is better known to modern readers in its nineteenth- and twentieth-century racist usage. The term was borrowed from Sanskrit by the Comte de Gobineau in the nineteenth century to refer to a supposed "Aryan race" responsible for all world progress, with the Germanic peoples as the "purest" of the Aryans. In the twentieth century the national socialists in Germany adopted the idea and used it as a basis for their elimination of those they considered non-Aryan peoples.

[3] Parasher 1991: 76. Parasher provides by far the most comprehensive and historically sensitive study of the term *mleccha* in early Indian discourse. See also Thapar 1971. On the similar use of *barbarian* in Greek and subsequent Western languages, see Jones 1971.

[4] *Ramayana* 2.1.18–19, 24–26, translation by Sheldon Pollock (1986). Throughout this chapter I use the excellent translations of Robert Goldman and the Ramayana Translation Consortium, available now for the first five of seven volumes of the epic. See Goldman 1984; Pollock 1986, 1991; Lefeber 1994; and Goldman and Goldman 1996.

[5] Descriptions of the sages and their ashrams in the Dandaka Forest are in *Ramayana*, book 3, chaps. 1–11, and elsewhere. See Pollock 1991.

[6] Kosambi [1956] 1975: 313. See also Kosambi 1965: 166–76; and Schwartzberg [1978] 1992: 164 on Brahman pioneers.

[7] Goldman (1984: 26–27) provides references to some of this scholarship. On the persistence of the equation of Indian tribals and monkeys, see Lutgendorf 2007.

CHAPTER 5

[1] For Yajnavalkya, see Goodall 1996: 293–337. Lingat 1973 still provides the best general overview of this genre of orthodox Sanskrit literature.

[2] Gordon 2008 offers an accessible and excellent overview of this Asiatic world through a series of vignettes. For the earlier portions of the period, Grousset 1971 provides a fine appreciation of the Buddhist-oriented Asian "golden age" that culminated around 700 CE. Whitfield 1999 evokes the world of Silk Road life during the period 750–1000. Ghosh 1994 brilliantly explores the old world of long-distance trade and adventure around 1100. For the history of South Asia for the period from 1000 on, with much attention devoted to larger geopolitical contexts, see Asher and Talbot 2006. Chaudhuri 1990 is an important work on the organization of the Indian Ocean trade prior to Portuguese and European intervention.

Suggestions for
Further Reading

Asher, Catherine B., and Cynthia Talbot. 2006. *India before Europe.* Cambridge: Cambridge University Press.

Begley, Vimala. 1996. Changing Perceptions of Arikamedu. In *The Ancient Port of Arikamedu: New Excavations and Researches, 1989–1992.* Memoires Archeologiques, vol. 22, 1–39. Pondichery: École Française d'Extrême-Orient.

Begley, Vimala, and Richard Daniel DePuma. 1991. *Rome and India: The Ancient Sea Trade.* Madison: University of Wisconsin Press.

Beteille, Andre. 1980. On the Concept of Tribe. *International Social Science Journal* 34, no. 4: 827–30.

Bulliet, Richard W. 1975. *The Camel and the Wheel.* Cambridge: Harvard University Press.

Bullis, Douglas. 1999. *The Mahavamsa: The Great Chronicle of Sri Lanka Originally Written by Thera Mahanama-sthavira.* Fremont, CA: Asian Humanities Press.

Casson, Lionel. 1984. *Ancient Trade and Society.* Detroit: Wayne State University Press.

———. 1989. *The Periplus Maris Erythraei: Text with Introduction, Translation, and Commentary.* Princeton: Princeton University Press.

Chanda, Nayan. 2007. *Bound Together: How Traders, Preachers, Adventurers, and Warriors Shaped Globalization.* New Haven: Yale University Press.

Chaudhuri, K. N. 1990. *Asia before Europe: Economy and Civilisation of the Indian Ocean from the Rise of Islam to 1750.* Cambridge: Cambridge University Press.

Ch'en, Kenneth K. S. 1964. *Buddhism in China: A Historical Survey.* Princeton: Princeton University Press.

Clough, Bradley S. n.d. "Encounters and Exchanges between Buddhism and Iranian Religion and Culture during the Kusana Period." Paper presented at Columbia University, New York.

Coedes, Georges. [1944] 1968. *The Indianized States of Southeast Asia.* Translated by Susan Brown Cowing. Honolulu: East-West Center Press.

Coomaraswamy, A. K. 1927. Origin of the Buddha Image. *Art Bulletin* 9:286–329.

Cowell, E. B. 1957. *The Jataka, or Stories of the Buddha's Former Lives*. London: Luzac.

Czuma, Stanislaw J. 1985. *Kushan Sculpture: Images from Early India*. Cleveland: Cleveland Museum of Art.

Dalby, Andrew. 2000. *Dangerous Tastes: The Story of Spices*. Berkeley: University of California Press.

Davis, Richard H. 2004. The Cultural Background of Hindutva. In *India Briefing*, edited by Philip Oldenberg and Alyssa Ayres, 107–139. New York: Asia Society.

Devadoss, Manohar. 1997. *Green Well Years*. Chennai: East-West Books.

Doniger, Wendy, and Brian K. Smith, trans. 1991. *The Laws of Manu*. London: Penguin.

Foucher, Alfred. 1917. The Greek Origin of the Image of the Buddha. In *The Beginnings of Buddhist Art and Other Essays in Indian and Central-Asian Archaeology*, 111–37. Paris: Paul Geuther.

Geiger, Wilhelm. 1908. *The Mahavamsa*. Pali Text Society Publications, vol. 63. London: Pali Text Society.

————. 1912. *The Mahavamsa, or The Great Chronicle of Ceylon*. Pali Text Society Translation Series, no.3. London: Pali Text Society.

Gernet, Jacques. [1972] 1996. *A History of Chinese Civilization*. 2nd ed. Translated by J. R. Foster and Charles Hartman. Cambridge: Cambridge University Press.

Ghosh, Amitav. 1994. *In an Antique Land*. New York: Vintage.

Giles, H. A. [1923] 1956. *The Travels of Fa-hsien (399–414 A.D.), or Record of the Buddhist Kingdoms*. London: Routledge and Kegan Paul.

Glover, I. C. 1989. *Early Trade between India and Southeast Asia: A Link in the Development of a World Trading System*. Occasional Papers, vol. 16. Hull: Center for South-East Asian Studies, University of Hull.

Goldman, Robert P., trans. 1984. *The Ramayana of Valmiki: An Epic of Ancient India.* Vol. 1: *Balakanda*. Princeton: Princeton University Press.

Goldman, Robert P., and Sally J. Sutherland Goldman. 1996. *The Ramayana of Valmiki: An Epic of Ancient India.* Vol. 5: *Sundarakanda*. Princeton: Princeton University Press.

Goodall, Dominic. 1996. *Hindu Scriptures with New Translations*. Berkeley: University of California Press.

Gordon, Stewart. 2008. *When Asia Was the World: Traveling Merchants, Scholars, Warriors, and Monks Who Created the "Riches of the East."* Philadelphia: Da Capo.

Grousset, Rene. [1929] 1971. *In the Footsteps of the Buddha*. Translated by J. A. Underwood. New York: Grossman.

Hall, Kenneth R. 1985. *Maritime Trade and State Development in Early Southeast Asia*. Honolulu: University of Hawai'i Press.

Hansen, Valerie. 2000. *The Open Empire: A History of China to 1600*. New York: Norton.

Hart, George L., and Hank Heifetz. 2002. *The Four Hundred Songs of War and Wisdom: An Anthology of Poems from Classical Tamil, the Purananuru*. New York: Columbia University Press.

Hartel, Herbert. 1982. *Along the Ancient Silk Routes: Central Asian Art from the West Berlin State Museums*. New York: Metropolitan Museum of Art.

Horner, I. B., trans. 1963. *Milinda's Questions*. Sacred Books of the Buddhists, vols. 22, 23. London: Luzac.

Huntington, Samuel P. 1996. *The Clash of Civilizations and the Remaking of World Order*. New York: Simon and Schuster.

Inden, Ronald. 1990. *Imagining India*. Oxford: Basil Blackwell.

Ingholt, Harald. 1957. *Gandharan Art in Pakistan*. New York: Pantheon.

Jones, Horace Leonard, trans. 1917. *The Geography of Strabo*. Loeb Classical Library, 8 vols, nos. 49–50, 182, 196, 211, 223, 241, 267. London: Heinemann.

Jones, W. R. 1971. The Image of the Barbarian in Medieval Europe. *Comparative Studies in Society and History* 13, no. 4: 376–407.

Katz, Nathan. 2000. *Who Are the Jews of India?* Berkeley: University of California Press.

Khoroche, Peter. 1989. *Once the Buddha Was a Monkey: Arya Sura's Jatakamala*. Chicago: University of Chicago Press.

Kissinger, Henry. 1979. *The White House Years*. New York: Little, Brown and Company.

Kosambi, Damodar Dharmanand. 1965. *Ancient India: A History of Its Culture and Civilization*. New York: Pantheon.

————. [1956] 1975. *An Introduction to the Study of Indian History*. 2nd ed. Bombay: Popular Prakashan.

Kulke, Hermann, and Dietmar Rothermund. 1986. *A History of India*. London: Routledge.

Lamotte. Etienne. 1988. *History of Indian Buddhism: From the Origins to the Saka Era*. Translated by Sara Webb-Boin. Publications de l'Institut Orientaliste de Louvain, vol. 36. Louvain-la-Neuve: Institut Orientaliste.

Lefeber, Rosalind. 1994. *The Ramayana of Valmiki: An Epic of Ancient India*. Vol. 4: *Kiskindakanda*. Edited by Robert P. Goldman. Princeton: Princeton University Press.

Lingat, Robert. 1973. *The Classical Law of India*. Translated by J. Duncan M. Derrett. Berkeley: University of California Press.

Liu, Xinru. 1988. *Ancient India and Ancient China: Trade and Religious Exchanges, A.D. 1–600*. Delhi: Oxford University Press.

————. 1998. *The Silk Road: Overland Trade and Cultural Interactions in Eurasia*. Washington, DC: American Historical Association.

Lutgendorf, Philip. 2007. *Hanuman's Tale: The Messages of a Divine Monkey*. Oxford: Oxford University Press.

Majumdar, R. C. 1985. *Champa: History and Culture of an Indian Colonial Kingdom in the Far East, 2nd–16th Century A.D.* Delhi: Gian Publishing House.

McNeill, William H. 1987. The Eccentricity of Wheels, or Eurasian Transportation in Historical Perspective. *American Historical Review* 92, no. 5: 1111–26.

Meile, Pierre. 1940. Les yavanas dans l'Inde tamoule. *Journal asiatique* 232:85–123.

Narain, A. K. 1957. *The Indo-Greeks*. Oxford: Clarendon.

Nehru, Lolita. 1989. *Origins of the Gandharan Style: A Study of Contributory Influences*. Delhi: Oxford University Press.

Panicker, Geevarghese. 2001. St. Thomas and the Thomas Tradition. In *A Dictionary of Asian Christianity*, edited by Scott W. Sunquist, 724–25. Grand Rapids, MI: Eerdmans.

Parasher, Aloka. 1991. *Mlecchas in Early India: A Study in Attitudes towards Outsiders up to AD 600*. New Delhi: Munshiram Manoharlal.

Poceski, Mario. 2004. Huayan Jing. In *Encyclopedia of Buddhism*, edited by Robert E. Buswell, 2 vols., 1:340–41. New York: Thomson-Gale.

Pollock, Sheldon. 1996. The Sanskrit Cosmopolis, 300–1300: Transculturation, Vernacularization, and the Question of Ideology. In *Ideology and Status of Sanskrit*, edited by Jan E. M. Houben, 197–247. Leiden: Brill.

————. 2006. *The Language of the Gods in the World of Men: Sanskrit, Culture, and Power in Premodern India*. Berkeley: University of California Press.

Pollock, Sheldon, trans. 1986. *The Ramayana of Valmiki: An Epic of Ancient India*. Vol. 2: *Ayodhyakanda*. Edited by Robert P. Goldman. Princeton: Princeton University Press.

————. 1991. *The Ramayana of Valmiki: An Epic of Ancient India*. Vol. 3: *Aranyakanda*. Edited by Robert P. Goldman. Princeton: Princeton University Press.

Przyluski, Jean. 1925. La princess a l'odeur du poisson et la Nagi dans les traditions de l'Asie orientale. In *Etudes asiatiques*, 2:265–84. Publications de École Française d'Extrême-Orient, vol. 20. Hanoi: École Française d'Extrême-Orient.

Raghavan, V. 1980. *The Ramayana Tradition in Asia*. New Delhi: Sahitya Akademi.

Ray, Himanshu Prabha. 2003. *The Archaeology of Seafaring in Ancient South Asia.* Cambridge: Cambridge University Press.

Reynolds, Frank. 1972. The Two Wheels of Dhamma: A Study of Early Buddhism. In *The Two Wheels of Dhamma: Essays on the Theravada Tradition in India and Ceylon*, edited by Bardwell L. Smith, 6–30. AAR Studies in Religion, vol. 3. Chambersburg, PA: American Academy of Religion.

Reynolds, Frank E., and Charles Hallisey. 1987. Buddhism: An Overview. In *Encyclopedia of Religion*, edited by Mircea Eliade, 2:334–51. New York: Macmillan.

Rhys Davids, T. W., and Hermann Oldenberg. 1881. *Vinaya Texts, Vol. 1.* Sacred Books of the East, vol. 13. 3 vols. Oxford: Clarendon.

Richman, Paula, ed. 1991. *Many Ramayanas: The Diversity of a Narrative Tradition in South Asia.* Berkeley: University of California Press.

Rosenfield, John M. 1967. *The Dynastic Arts of the Kushans.* California Studies in the History of Art, no. 6, edited by Walter Horn. Berkeley: University of California Press.

———. 2006. Prologue: Some Debating Points on Gandharan Buddhism and Kusana History. In *Gandharan Buddhism: Archaeology, Art, Texts*, edited by Pia Brancaccio and Kurt Behrendt, 9–37. Vancouver: University of British Columbia Press.

Ryan, James D. 2005. *Civakacintamani: The Hero Civakan, the Gem That Fulfills All Wishes, by Tiruttakkatevar.* Fremont, CA: Jain.

Sattar, Arshia. 1996. *The Ramayana.* New Delhi: Penguin Books India.

Schopen, Gregory. 1988–89. On Monks, Nuns and "Vulgar" Practices: The Introduction of the Image Cult into Indian Buddhism. *Artibus Asiae* 49, nos. 1–2: 153–68.

Schwartzberg, Joseph E. [1978] 1992. *A Historical Atlas of South Asia.* 2d ed. New York: Oxford University Press.

Selby, Martha Ann. 2008. Representations of the Foreign in Classical Tamil Literature. In *Ancient India in Its Wider World*, edited by Grant Parker and Carla M. Sinopoli, 79–90. Ann Arbor: Centers for South and Southeast Asian Studies, University of Michigan.

Sen, Amartya. 2005. *The Argumentative Indian: Writings on Indian History, Culture, and Identity.* New York: Picador.

Shaffer, Lynda Norene. 1996. *Maritime Southeast Asia to 1500.* Armonk, NY: M. E. Sharpe.

Sidebotham, Steven E. 1986. *Roman Economic Policy in the Erythra Thalassa, 30 B.C.– A.D. 217.* Mnemosyne, vol. 91. Leiden: Brill.

Smith, Bardwell L. 1978. *Religion and Legitimation of Power in Sri Lanka.* Chambersburg, PA: Anima.

Speyer, J. S. 1895. *The Jatakamala, or Garland of Birth-Stories.* Sacred Books of the Buddhists, vol. 1. London: Henry Frowde.

Tawney, C. H. 1895. *The Kathakosa, or Treasury of Stories.* Oriental Translation Fund, vol. 6. London: Royal Asiatic Society.

————. 1924–28. *The Ocean of Story, Being C. H. Tawney's Translation of Somadeva's* Kathasaritsagara. 10 vols. London: C. J. Sawyer.

Teiser, Stephen T. 2005. Buddhism: Buddhism in China. In *Encyclopedia of Religion,* edited by Lindsay Jones, 2d ed., 2:1160–69. Detroit: Thomson Gale.

Thapar, Romila. 1971. The Image of the Barbarian in Early India. *Comparative Studies in Society and History* 13, no. 4: 408–36.

————. 2002. *Early India.* Berkeley: University of California Press.

Todaro, Dale. 1987. Kumarajiva. In *Encyclopedia of Religion,* edited by Mircea Eliade, 8:398–400. New York: Macmillan.

Tsiang, Katherine R. 2003. The Cult of Buddhist Relics and the Silk Road. In *The Glory of the Silk Road: Art from Ancient China,* edited by Li Jian, 49–55. Dayton: Dayton Art Museum.

Van Buitenen, J. A. B. 1959. *Tales of Ancient India.* Chicago: University of Chicago Press.

Vogel, J. Ph. 1930. *La sculpture de Mathura.* Ars Asiatica, vol. 15. Paris: Les editions G. Van Oest.

Vyas, Shantikumar Nanooram. 1967. *India in the Ramayana Age: A Study of the Social and Cultural Conditions in Ancient India as Described in Valmiki's* Ramayana. Delhi: Atma Ram and Sons.

Warmington, E. H. [1928] 1974. *The Commerce between the Roman Empire and India.* 2d ed. London: Curzon.

Waterfield, Robin, trans. 1998. *The Histories of Herodotus.* Oxford: Oxford University Press.

Wheatley, Paul. 1961. *The Golden Khersonese: Studies in the Historical Geography of the Malay Peninsula before A.D. 1500.* Kuala Lumpur: University of Malaya Press.

————. 1983. *Nagara and Commandery: Origins of the Southeast Asian Urban Traditions.* Research Papers, vols. 207–8. Chicago: Department of Geography, University of Chicago.

Wheeler, Robert Eric Mortimer. 1954. *Rome beyond the Imperial Frontiers.* London: Bell.

Whitfield, Susan. 1999. *Life along the Silk Road.* London: Murray.

Wolters, O. W. 1982. *History, Culture, and Region in Southeast Asian Perspective.* Singapore: Institute of Southeast Asian Studies.

Young, Gary K. 2001. *Rome's Eastern Trade: International Commerce and Imperial Policy, 31 B.C.–A.D. 305.* London: Routledge.

Yun-hua, Jan. 1987. Fa-hsien. In *Encyclopedia of Religion*, edited by Mircea Eliade, 5:245–46. New York: Macmillan.

Zürcher, Erik. 1967. The Yueh-Chin and Kanishka in the Chinese Sources. In *From Alexander to Kanishka*, edited by A. K. Narain, 72–104. Monographs of the Department of Ancient Indian History, Culture and Archaeology, no. 1. Varanasi: Banaras Hindu University.

———. 1972. *The Buddhist Conquest of China: The Spread and Adaptation of Buddhism in Early Medieval China.* Leiden: Brill.

Zvelebil, Kamil. 1956. The Yavanas in Old Tamil Literature. In *Charisteria Orientalia*, edited by Felix Tauer, Vera Kubickova, and Ivan Hrbek, 401–9. Prague: Ceskoslovenske Akademie.